CARMARTHENSHIRE COAST
& GOWER CIRCULAR WALKS

Hazards and Problems
Take Notice, Take Care

The author and the publishers stress that walkers should be aware of the dangers that may occur on all walks.

- check local weather forecast before walking; do not walk up into mist or low clouds
- use local OS maps side by side with walking guides
- wear walking boots and clothing
- do not take any unnecessary risks – conditions can change suddenly and can vary from season to season
- take special care when accompanied by children or dogs
- when walking on roads, ensure that you are conspicuous to traffic from either direction

CARMARTHENSHIRE COAST & GOWER CIRCULAR WALKS

Paul Williams

Carreg
Gwalch

First edition: 2000
Revised edition: 2011
© Text: Paul Williams

ISBN: 978-1-84524-142-1

Cover Design: Alan Jones

First published in 2000 by Gwasg Carreg Gwalch

Revised edition published in 2011 by Llygad Gwalch,
Ysgubor Plas, Llwyndyrys, Pwllheli, Gwynedd LL53 6NG.
☎: 01758 750432 📠: 01758 750438
✉: books@carreg-gwalch.com
web site: www.carreg-gwalch.com

CONTENTS

Features

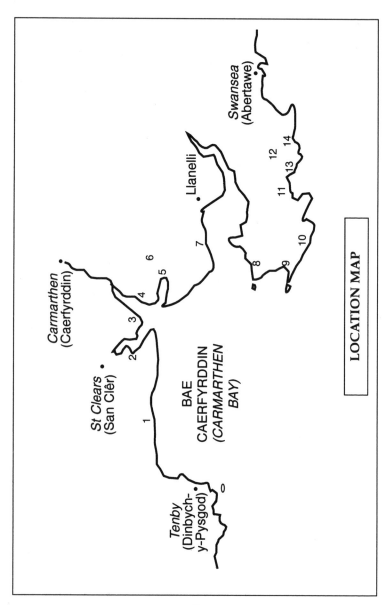

LOCATION MAP

Swansea
(Abertawe)

Llanelli

Carmarthen
(Caerfyrddin)

St Clears
(San Clêr)

Tenby
(Dinbych-
y-Pysgod)

BAE
CAERFYRDDIN
(CARMARTHEN
BAY)

0 1 2 3 4 5 6 7 8 9 10 11 12 13 14

8

INTRODUCTION

Out and About

One of the aims of this guide is simplicity. Walks are easy to follow, and clear directions are given. Another aim is variety. Walks have been selected that will highlight both Carmarthenshire's (Sir Gaer) and the Gower peninsula's (Penrhyn Gŵyr) outstanding landscape beauty and history. The exact location for the start point of each walk is given, and how to get there – however as the walks are circular they may be joined at any convenient point. Relevant bus and train details are included, though not all public services will operate on Sundays. Check with Information Centres or bus and train stations for full details. First Cymru operate summer Sunday buses around Gower. There is adequate parking space at the start of each walk, and precise details are given.

Walks vary in length from 2 miles/3.5 kilometres to 11 miles/17.5 kilometres. The routes utilise public footpaths, bridleways and the occasional permissive path. They are well maintained, and clearly signposted and waymarked – a yellow arrow or waymark indicating a public footpath, a blue one a bridleway. The Cydweli/Kidwelly area offers several distinctive green stiles! Many people are uncertain of how long a walk of e.g. 7 miles/11 kilometres would take. As a rough guide an average walker would expect to cover 3 miles/4.75 kilometres an hour over level ground, on the ascent an hour for every 2000 feet/600 metres. Sketch maps for each walk are provided, the majority based on the 1:25 000 OS (Ordnance Survey) map series; however they can be no substitute for the real thing. The 1:50 000 Landranger series (1.25 inches = 1 mile/2 centimetres = 1 kilometre) cover the area in 2 maps: Tenby, and Swansea and Gower. Those preferring greater detail will wish to acquire the 1:25 000 series (2.5 inches = 1 mile/4 centimetres = 1 kilometre) now available in the Explorer edition (and replacing the old green cover Pathfinder series): 177 Carmarthen & Kidwelly, and 10 Gower. The relevant maps for each walk are listed.

The grading system used is largely self-explanatory. Easy walks involve short walks over easy terrain, with little variation in contour. Moderate may have 1 or 2 short steep sections, with a little more variety in landscape, whilst strenuous will involve longer distances, with perhaps greater sections of ascent and descent, and over different types of terrain e.g. heather, woodland paths etc. Points of interest are included that are designed to give a quick snapshot of a particular area and what gives a place, in landscape or historical terms, it's own brand of uniqueness. Under facilities are listed public telephones, toilets, cafés and pubs, shops and youth hostels. Most small towns and many farms will offer B&B – check with Information Centres if you are interested. Also listed under facilities are any additional places of interest in the neighbourhood e.g. wildlife parks, heritage centres and nature reserves.

Finally a word of warning. Footpaths get muddy, and cliffs can be dangerous. Take care! Ensure you have adequate clothing, and the proper footwear, ie boots or stout shoes, for each walk. Follow the Country Code!

Landscape and Culture

The Gower peninsula and the Carmarthenshire and Pembrokeshire coast, together with Caldey Island, frame Carmarthen Bay. Into the bay feeds the Three Rivers system of Taf, Tywi and Gwendraeth, with to the east the drowned river valley of the river Loughor (Afon Llwchwr) and it's continuation in the Burry Inlet. The magnificent southern limestone edge of Gower faces out across the Bristol Channel to the English West Country of Devon and Cornwall. The area is one of great habitat diversity, with the western cliffs of Carmarthenshire giving way to sand and estuary, only to be succeeded by the great cliffs of Gower, with it's wide sandy bays.

Carmarthenshire (Sir Gâr) comprises some one thousand square miles. To the west of Carmarthen (Caerfyrddin) the soft improved agricultural grasslands meet the cliffs at Marros and Pendine, and again at Wharley Point. Areas of unimproved grassland are rare, surviving only as common land; south east of Carmarthen, where agriculture has been less intense, there are greater areas. Much of the explanation for this is due to the underlying geology. Central Carmarthenshire is a plateau of Old Red Sandstone, edged on it's western side by a belt of limestone by Pendine, and then further to the west a belt of millstone grit. South eastern Carmarthenshire lies at the edge of the great South Wales coalfield, Pennant sandstone alternating with the coal measures, with a limestone belt at it's north western edge running through Mynydd-y-Garreg, with adjacent to it on it's southern flank a belt of millstone grit by Kidwelly. To the south of the coalfield there is another belt of millstone grit running across the neck of Gower

(Gŵyr). Many of the miners who worked the coalfield, particularly in the Llanelli area, supplemented their living from small holdings. Many of these surviving unimproved pastures are now under threat from open cast mining – there is a large area of open cast between Pont-iets and Trimsaran, to the east of Kidwelly. Areas of open common survive on the untilled millstone grits of Gower at Clyne, Fairwood and Pengwern, and at Welsh Moor – many of Gower's small livestock and dairy farms have ancient commons grazing rights. Gower's flora-rich limestone grassland is nationally known – many see Gower's limestone as it's true heart, and the southern area of the peninsula receives many more summer visitors than it's less well known but equally rewarding northern shore.

Gower's small area – it is roughly 19 miles long and 3 to 8 miles wide – has a complex geology. The Devonian Old Red Sandstone and younger Carboniferous limestone and millstone grit beds were laid down horizontally one on the other over a period of a hundred million years, and then subjected to immense upheaval during the Armorican mountain building movements. The land was buckled into huge folds with the limestone and millstone grit curved into an arc over the Old Red Sandstone. Following extensive weathering the surface of Gower was then levelled off. This is not the final chapter in the formation of the land surface however. As recently as three million years ago (almost yesterday in geological terms) the sea invaded South Wales, to fall by

progressive stages creating in the process a series of marine platforms – the lowest at 200 feet (62 metres) cut about one million years ago. The Old Red Sandstone heath ridges of Cefn Bryn, Rhossili Downs and Llanmadoc hill resisted this last erosion. Further incursions, this time of ice, occurred as sheets of the great Irish Sea glacier rolled, scratched and rumbled across the surface; the last glacial maximum occurring 18,000 years ago.

Little now remains of the post glacial woodlands that once covered Carmarthenshire and Gower. Cut down over the centuries not only for pasture but also to flush out Welsh rebels during the Norman occupation they survive best in the valleys that cut into the landscape, and where their steep sides have proved them unmanageable to agriculture. In Gower, the Bishopston and Ilston valleys, and Green Cwm by Parkmill, give a flavour of how it must once have been. A considerable amount of the woodland was further devastated during the two world wars; much of what remained was replanted with conifers. As early as the 1920s Corsican pine was being planted at Pen-bre (Pembrey).

Carmarthenshire (Sir Gaerfyrddin) in particular is rich in it's freshwater rivers. It may be that the ancestors of these rivers were superimposed on the chalk beds formed by marine transgressions in the Upper Cretaceous, however nothing now remains of the Mesozoic deposits apart from an outlier of the Triassic by Port Eynon. Examples of standing water are to be found at Witchett pool between Pendine and Laugharne Burrows, Ffrwd Fen by Pen-bre (Pembrey), Machynys ponds by Llanelli and Broad Pool on the edge of Cefn Bryn in Gower. Man-made examples are the disused canals in the Kidwelly and Burry Port area, Cwm Lliedi reservoir (which supplies Llanelli), Sandy Water Park Llanelli and at Oxwich in Gower. Many farms will have a pond, particularly in Gower where it seems every other pond has a heron at station, only to flap lazily away when aware of company.

Carmarthenshire has some 50 miles of coastline, much of it low lying; however it's current stability belies the fact that most of it has only formed since 1800, a large proportion of the dune system forming during the last 50 years. During medieval/early modern times Pendine and Laugharne Burrows were absent, the hills behind marking the coastline, estuaries were wider and Cefn Sidan sands were missing. There was an island off present day Llanelli, and a marsh stretched from Kidwelly to Pen-bre. There are extensive dunes at Whiteford and

Broughton/Llangenydd Burrows on the north western tip of Gower, with both Port Eynon and Oxwich Bays' sandy beaches backed by dunes. By contrast Rhossili's beach is backed by a stable shingle ridge. The Loughor (Llwchwr) estuary has the most extensive area of salt marsh in Wales, with further areas at the common estuary of the Three Rivers, and again at Oxwich national nature reserve.

The extensive mud flats, sand and saltmarsh of the Loughor (Llwchwr) estuary and the Burry Inlet are of international significance for waterfowl (waders and wildfowl). The area is a Ramsar site (so called after an international convention held on wetlands at Ramsar, Iran in 1971); it is also designated a Special Protection Area under the Wildlife and Countryside Act of 1981. At Penclacwydd, south-east of Llanelli, is the Wildlife and Wetlands Trust centre, with thousands of the world's rarest swans, geese and ducks on acres of ponds, lakes and saltmarsh. Perhaps the most exciting event in the area is the transformation of the former industrial dereliction of the inlet's north bank into the Millennium Coastal Park Llanelli. It stretches from the Loughor bridge to Pen-bre and includes 250 acres of wetland habitat, plus fishing lakes and community woodlands, as well as modern sports facilities. Major sites for seabird colonies are at Telpyn and Gilman Points by Pendine, and at Worms Head, the dragon tongue of Gower. Carmarthen Bay supports large numbers of common scoter – prior to the Sea Empress oil spill in 1996 numbers were as high as 31% of the national population.

Man makes his first appearance in Wales at Pontnewydd cave in North Wales during an interglacial period some 225,000/200,000 years ago, with finds of hand axes and early Neanderthal teeth. By comparison Britain's oldest sites giving up human remains date back to 500,000 to 400,000, years ago, with finds at Boxgrove and Swanscombe in south-eastern England. At Rhossili a single hand axe has been found dating back 125,000 years, and at Coygan cave near Laugharne tools of Neanderthal type have been dated back to an early glacial period of the last Ice Age some 45,000 years ago. The most spectacular discovery occurred in 1823 with the finding on Gower of the first modern human skeleton in Europe, The Red Lady of Paviland, dating back 26,000 years – by this time Neanderthal man had become extinct. Britain was not fully an island until circa 8,500 years ago, and South Wales would have been marginal land at the edge of Europe, with the Bristol Channel just a river in a wide plain. There would have been little in the way of settlement, but hyenas as well as man would have used the limestone caves strung out along Gower's shore, and the hyena dens have given up their secret stores of bones of mammoth and woolly rhinoceros, of reindeer and elephant, cave bear and cave lion.

With the end of the Ice Age, and the retreat of the ice sheets some 10,000 years ago, the climate improved and the sea levels began to rise; the subarctic tundra gave way to birch and pine forest and then progressively to broad-leaf. The forests attracted deer, wild pig and cattle, and new tools of bone and antler were developed for hunting, with the rich coastal areas offering attractive fishing grounds, with sea birds and wildfowl as part of the menu. Temporary settlements gradually gave way to more permanent sites, and there is evidence of the herding of red deer and the harvesting of fruit and nuts. Settlement sites were created in upland and coastal areas; there is evidence of a stone chipping floor at Burry Holms in Gower, and of possible settlement at Coygan cave Laugharne. This mesolithic hunter-gatherer society gradually gave way circa 4,000 BC to the neolithic era.

With the neolithic age came a new relationship with the land; the given environment was modified to include domesticated wheat and barley, sheep, cattle and goats. This meant the clearance of the woodland, and fixed settlement, a settled home in the natural landscape of the mesolithic era. It has long been heralded that this neolithic farming revolution was introduced into Britain by incomers, with the mesolithic inhabitants forced into the margins, but perhaps it was a more a mixture of the migration of ideas and settlers that forged the new society. Little survives of their day to day settlements, made of wood (only in the Orkneys at the tip of Scotland did the climate require stone). However the landscape they inhabited is marked by ritual reminders of their presence in the great stone burial chambers. Perhaps with kinship with the land came the need to express that kinship through ritual possession of the landscape through reminders of their ancestors – longevity of kin given expression in the burial mound, the symbol of territory and ownership of landscape.

There are fine examples of their burial chambers at Ragwen Point by Pendine, and in Gower the Sweyn's Howes on the slopes of Rhossili Downs, at Penmaen Burrows by Three Cliffs Bay and at Parc le Breos in Green Cwm. Perhaps the most famous is Arthur's Stone, sometimes known as Maen Ceti. It has been argued that the late neolithic early Bronze Age eras heralded the development of a new ideology and

14

society associated with the rising and setting sun and moon. Along with the decline in monumental burial chambers – they were replaced by single round burial chambers built on higher and more visible ground than their predecessors, as on Rhossili Downs – went the building of stone circles, henges and stone alignments; these processional alignments could be interpreted as processional journeys from death to the afterlife. There seems to have been a desertion of settlements and a re-establishment of cleared woodland, though the agricultural system appears to have remained stable. Arthur's Stone has long been argued as a neolithic burial chamber, but it has been suggested as a later Bronze Age site; the angle of it's stone has been found to point to the polar north star, whose constellation is the Little Bear, smaller companion to the constellation of the Great Bear. It may be more than coincidence that in Welsh, Arth Fawr, close to the pronunciation of the name Arthur, means in English Great Bear. It is believed that the arrival of the Bronze Age (2,000 to 600 BC) was heralded by the immigration of the Beaker people from Europe (so called because of their characteristic decorated pottery drinking vessels), carrying knowledge of copper and bronze, and it's use in weaponry and jewellery, but again as with the neolithic, it may have been as much a movement of ideas and trade.

The late Bronze Age witnessed a deterioration in climate and widespread movements of population in Europe. Upland areas were abandoned, and for the first time pressure on farmland resulted in the building of defensive settlements. Strategic sites favoured were coastal headlands and hilltops; this pattern continued with the gradual development of iron working, and as the Iron Age progresses society took on a more aggressive face – the larger forts perhaps exercising some control over the smaller defended settlements with regional grouping forming the basis of future tribal areas. North Gower has two excellent hilltop forts, the Bulwark on Llanmadoc hill, and Cil Ifor, dating from 100 BC and, at 8 acres, the largest in the peninsula. Gilman Point by Pendine makes full use of it's coastal setting and natural defensive position. One long standing theory has it that it was at the beginning of the Iron Age that the Celts arrived in numbers in Britain, speaking the ancestors of the modern Celtic languages. However it is also argued that there was no major influx of people and that the Celtic languages in Britain date back to the early Bronze Age. Society as it developed is thought to have come under the influence of the Celtic mores of Iron Age Europe.

The Roman period begins with Julius Caesar's landing on the Kent coastline in 55 BC. By AD 78 the conquest of Wales was complete. In south-west Wales the Demetae tribe offered little opposition to Roman rule, and no fort or road west of the administrative tribal capital of Moridunum, modern day Carmarthen, has been found. The impact of Romanisation – money, roads, towns, markets and the villa with it's modern farming techniques – on the area is slight; there was a road connecting Moridunum with forts at Loughor and Neath. In Gower, within the area of the more aggressive Silures of south-east Wales, the remains of a mosaic floor of a Roman villa at Oystermouth have been found.

With the collapse of Roman rule in the early 5th century the pattern of small scale farming continued, much as it had done during the Iron Age and Roman times, with services and obligations owed by smaller farmers and bondsmen to the nobles. However the removal of a central authority left the land open to raids, first by the Irish – an Irish dynasty was most probably in power in west Wales by the end of the 5th century – and later by the Vikings. The years 400 to 600 were crucial to the formation of Wales as a country, as it was to the Scottish and English nations, and it is the fortunes of the early kingdoms and their rulers that give the period the political flavour of the age. By the mid 10th century it was possible, if only temporarily, for Hywel Dda (the Good) to have added the kingdom of Deheubarth (Ceredigion [Cardiganshire], Penfro [Pembrokeshire], Caerfyrddin [Carmarthenshire] and Gŵyr [Gower]) to the northern and eastern kingdoms of Gwynedd and Powys, and to have consolidated the Law of Wales, quite possibly at a meeting held at Hendy-gwyn (Whitland) in Carmarthenshire.

Evidence of early medieval settlement has been found at Coygan near Laugharne (a much favoured place throughout early history), but sites are rare. The 5th and 6th centuries was the Age of the Saints, when peregrini, travelling monks from Europe and Ireland, helped consolidate the hold of Christianity in Wales and lay the foundations of the Celtic church. Central to the local community was the *llan*, so common a feature of Welsh place names, this being an enclosure, often circular (and often making use of an already circular site) for burial. Llansaint's churchyard is of this type. Other early Christian evidence derives from the many Christian stones, inscribed with the names of

16

the aristocracy, and marking the site of their graves. Some of the earliest are in Latin and /or ogham – ogham an Irish script of cut notches along the edge of the stone to indicate spelling, an indication of early Irish presence in the area. Ogham had ceased by 600, later stones being in Latin. More elaborate stones, decorated with linework and fine crosses, may have marked church property. There are memorial stones to two chieftains of Irish origin set in the churchwalls at Llansaint church and another, at Llanmadoc, has been set into the window sill of the church. Laugharne's 9th/10th century disk-headed cross has been moved from the churchyard into the church. There is at Scotts Bay near Llansteffan a medieval well in good preservation where a 6th century hermit Anthony used the waters to bless pilgrims on their way to and from St David's.

The Norman conquest of 1066 changed the face of Wales. Initially Rhys ap Tewdwr managed to retain his rule over Deheubarth, though acknowledging overlordship to William the Conqueror who crossed his lands in 1081 on a 'pilgrimage' to St David's. However after Rhys' death a series of lordships were established in this south-western corner of the Marches of Wales. In the commote, or district of Gŵyr (Gower), the Normans concentrated on the fertile lowlands building castles at Loughor, Swansea and Oystermouth protecting the neck and peninsula, leaving north Gower and it's extension to the south Wales foothills as Welsh Gower. Castles were built at Carmarthen, Laugharne, Llansteffan and Kidwelly, sited not only on strategic high points, but also close to the rivers and sea-lanes. Early castles were earth and timber, either ringwork as at Penmaen Gower, or motte and bailey, and subject to constant attack. With consolidation of power and the continuing need for defence, stone was used – Kidwelly in the concentric style is one of the finest and most impregnable. Until Edward I's conquest of Wales in 1282, Wales outside the Marches was allowed to retain it's separate identity. Thereafter, apart from the Owain Glyndŵr uprising in the early 15th century, the Welsh were ruled under a watchful Norman eye.

To serve the lords in the castle traders and craftsmen settled close by, and in time these communities were granted trade rights and privileges, and later charters confirming borough status. This pattern of urban growth formed the basis of the urban structure of Wales until the Industrial Revolution. Carmarthen was, by the late 16th century, *the chiefe citie of the country*, with Kidwelly and Swansea (Abertawe) among the first rank. Norman society was nothing if not rigid; at the head of it's structure was God, with the King and villein all bound to those above by duty. The expression of that social order was in land, the great estates of the Norman lords, and the obligations of their feudal tenants. The most fertile land was given to their followers, the Welsh were forced to the uplands where they were allowed to keep their customs and law, whilst in the new urban areas settlement was restricted, at least initially, to the non Welsh. In Gower there were settlers from Devon and Somerset and at Kidwelly Flemings. Of the medieval strip field system there are survivals at the Hugden Laugharne, and at the Vile Rhossili.

Inevitably the Normans found the Celtic church too independent and it was quickly remodelled along Continental lines. St David's became one of four Welsh dioceses, with outlying churches organised into a parish system; new churches with defensive towers being built on the old llanau, and the dedications to Celtic saints usually being removed and rededicated to Roman ones. Celtic monasticism was also tied to Europe and European orders – a new Cistercian monastery was established at Whitland (Hendy-gwyn) in 1140. Other established religious houses that were founded included the Knights Hospitallers, with their Welsh commandery at Slebech in Pembrokeshire. Norman lords were quick to grant manors for income to the new houses and orders – in Gower by the late 12th century churches at Rhossili, Llandimore and Llanrhidian had been given to the Knights Hospitallers, the manor of Llanmadoc to the Knights Templar, and the church at Llangenydd to the Norman abbey of St Taurin of Evereux.

By the time of the accession to the English throne in 1485 of Henry VII, born in nearby Pembroke Castle, society in the Marches and in Wales as a whole had become more peaceful and orderly. Castles could be modified to become comfortable manor houses, as at Oxwich and Weobley on Gower, and the Welsh gentry who had leant their support to Henry Tudor as he had taken to the field against Richard III at Bosworth were suitably rewarded. The Acts of Union of 1536-43 marked the political merger of Wales with England.

The years from the Acts of Union to 1770 have been characterised as the age of the gentry, of the rise of the yeoman farmer. It was they who received the bulk of economic surplus and who exercised control over the destiny of their fellow men. The Acts of Union had abolished the privileges of the Marches of Wales tying the fortunes of their lords to

those of Henry VIII's state. The dissolution of the monasteries in 1540 was similarly an exercise in asserting the authority of the Tudor state. Following the break with Rome the Church of England was established, but it is open to debate how wholeheartedly the new church was adopted. Given the Welsh nonconformist tradition it might be supposed that the mid 17th century sects of Puritanism may have had attractions; but again there seems to have been little initial appeal – perhaps it required the urban spark that the Industrial Revolution would bring. In Ilston cwm on Gower John Myles did establish the first Baptist church in Wales between 1649-60, but with the Restoration of Charles II he and his followers were forced into exile in America. It was during the Civil War that the castles saw their last moments of glory; however any which had served the Royalist cause, as did Swansea and Oystermouth, were quickly rendered defenceless by Cromwell's men after victory. Many were left to fade into obscurity, to find uses in later centuries as Romantic ruins.

The years from 1700 to 1850 witnessed an unprecedented two and half times growth in agricultural output in Britain as a whole. Coupled with this in Wales, as internationally, was a population growth. It has been estimated that in 1500 some 80% of the British population worked on the land, by 1800 this figure had dropped to 30% – the surplus absorbed by the quickening of the Industrial Revolution from the mid

18th century onwards. There had been local industry before the revolution; there were textile mills on Afon Gwendraeth Fach, and the Swansea area had a long industrial and maritime tradition. By 1820 however the area between Aberafan and Llanelli, part of the south Wales coalfield, produced 90% of Britain's copper and a large percentage of it's silver, lead and zinc. It was also the centre of the tinplate industry – tinplate was first used to can food in 1825. Once a sleepy village, Llanelli had, by 1835, a population of six thousand and it's night sky was lit by the roaring flames of industry.

In the early years of the 19th century the iron industry was pre-eminent in the economy of Wales, and it was on Welsh iron that the trains of the railway era ran – the first to be built in Wales opened in 1839 running from Llanelli to Pontarddulais. The railways replaced the canals and tramroads built by the early industrialists, men like Thomas Kymer who built Wales's first real commercial canal in the Kidwelly area from 1766-68. The Kidwelly and Llanelli canal, the most technically advanced in the area, had the ignominy of having rails laid along it's towpath. Alongside the railways came the expansion of harbours and docks at Burry Port and Llanelli, as at Swansea. The

smaller coastal ports, particularly on Gower where road conditions were dire, had long flourished – the sea was the main highway, not the land. For much of the 18th and 19th centuries the limestone of Gower's southern edge was quarried for export to Somerset and Devon for use as fertiliser on their limeless soils. The 18th and early 19th centuries were also the heyday of the smugglers, especially on Gower, where imports of spirits, salt, soap or tea found their way into nearly every household.

Though conditions for many in the new industrial towns were harsh and brutal (as they could be in rural areas) improvements in transport and the growth of urban centres offered increasing opportunities for the growth of popular Welsh politics, religion and culture from the 1870s onwards – Llanelli rugby football club was founded in 1875, Swansea's in 1874. However the modernisation of society and the economy also meant the gradual end of patterns of trade that had existed for centuries; the smaller coastal trading ports fell into disuse, and the agricultural fairs were replaced by marts close to urban centres. The railway age fostered the growth of tourism as an industry and, by the beginning of the 20th century, people were moving into rural areas whose only interest in the land was as a source of leisure not agriculture or industry.

Agriculture continued to modernise throughout the 20th century, with the introduction of subsidies early in the century, and post 1945 new technological innovations and the introduction of chemicals onto the land. The development of local government from the late 19th century onwards followed on from the rule of the squirearchy – Camarthenshire's county hall is at Carmarthen (Caerfyrddin); Gower, part of West Glamorgan, looks to Swansea. Gower was designated Britain's first Area of Outstanding Natural Beauty in May 1956, and contains within it three national nature reserves and two local nature reserves. With the closure of the coalfields and industrial decline has come a new initiative to refurbish the Llanelli area, and 2000 sees the opening of the Millennium Coastal Park – Carmarthenshire is also fortunate in being the location of the new National Botanical Gardens of Wales at Llanarthne near Carmarthen (Caerfyrddin). Appropriately Llanelli was host to the first National Eisteddfod of the new century; Carmarthenshire and Llanelli have always been strongholds of the Welsh language, unlike south Gower which, with it's Norman history is like neighbouring south Pembrokeshire across Carmarthen Bay – very much a little England beyond Wales. Inevitably as Wales enters the 21st century with a newly elected National Assembly, there will be fresh problems and solutions. In environmental terms there is the potential for the creation of new landscapes though genetically modified crops; there is the continuing problem of viewing Sites of Special Scientific Interest (SSSIs), the final sanctuary, as being expendable; and there is also the issue of the right to roam. However no doubt these concerns will be tempered by legislation and action.

Place Names

The study of place names is a fascinating branch of local history in it's own right, indicating geographical features (which may have vanished), patterns of former land ownership, forgotten buildings or former trades. However the current place name may be far removed from the original name, particularly where there is an anglicised form of an old Welsh name. Welsh place names are particularly expressive of geography, and can be highly poetic in combination. Some of the more common words are listed below:

Aber – river mouth, estuary	*Dinas* – hill fort
Afon – river	*Dôl* – meadow
Allt – slope	*Du/Ddu* – black
Ar – on, over	*Dŵr* – water
Bach/Fach – little	*Eglwys* – church
Barcud – kite	*Ffordd* – road
Bedd – grave	*Ffrwd* – stream, torrent
Bre - hill	*Ffynnon* – well
Bryn – hill	*Gelli* – grove
Bwlch – pass	*Glan* – river bank
Caer(au) – fort(s)	*Glas* – blue, green
Canol – middle, centre	*Gwaun* – moor, meadow
Capel – chapel	*Gwyn/Gwen* – white
Carn/Garn – cairn	*Gwynt* – wind
Carreg, pl cerrig – rock, stone	*Hafod* – summer dwelling
Castell – castle	*Hen* – old
Cefn – ridge	*Hendre* – winter dwelling
Cil – nook, source of stream	*Heol* – road
Clawdd – ditch	*Isaf* – lower
Coch – red	*Lan* – ascent
Coed – wood	*Llan, pl llannau* – church, village
Cors/Gors – bog, marsh	*Llyn* – lake
Craig – rock, cliff	*Llwybr* – path, track
Crib – ridge	*Llwyn* – grove, bush
Croes – cross	*Maen* – rock, stone
Cromlech(i) – burial mound(s)	*Maes* – field
Cwm – valley	*Marchog* – knight
Cwrw – beer	*Mawr/Fawr* – great, big
Cyhoeddus – public	*Melin* – mill
Dan – under	*Melyn* – yellow
Dau – two	*Moel/Foel* – bare topped hill
Deri – oak trees	*Mynydd* – mountain

Nant – brook, stream
Newydd – new
Ogof – cave
Parc – field, park
Pen – head, top
Penlan – top of hill
Pentre – village
Plas – hall
Pont – bridge
Porth – harbour
Pwll – pool
Rhiw – hill

Rhos – moorland
Rhyd – ford
Sidan – silk
Tafarn – inn
Traeth – beach
Tref – town, hamlet
Tŷ – house
Uchaf – upper
Y/Yr – the
Yn – in
Ynys – island
Ysgol - school

A few notes on pronunciation:

c – k (hard)
ch – as in lo*ch*
dd – th as in *th*at
f – v
ff – f
g – g (hard)
ll – pronounce l, keep tongue in position at roof of mouth, and hiss!
th – th as in *th*ink

There are 7 vowels, a, e, i, o, u, w and y. Pronunciation may be long or short.

w may be as in pool, or pull e.g. *cwm* (coom) – valley
y may be as in fun, or pin eg *y, yr* (u, ur) – the, *dyffryn* (dufrin) – valley

Many Welsh words change their pronunciation and spelling under certain circumstances eg the initial consonant of many words may soften: b to f, c to g, m to f, p to b etc. Common examples of mutations are bach (little) to fach, mawr (big) to fawr, porth (harbour) to borth. Such mutations can make tracing words through a dictionary a little problematic for the uninitiated!

Tourist Information Centres

Carmarthen – Lammas Street 01267 231557
Llanelli – Public Library, Vaughan Street 01554 772020
Mumbles – Oystermouth Square .01792 361302
Swansea – Plymouth Street (opp. Quadrant Bus Station) . .01792 468321

Further Walks

Carmarthen Bay Coastal Path.
Links Amroth and the Pembrokeshire Coast Path with Pendine. Will extend to Laugharne.

Cwm Lliedi Reservoir.
Situated just to the north west of Llanelli there is a pleasant circular walk around the reservoir.

The Gower Way.
Inaugurated in 1998 the Gower Way will link Penlle'r Castell in 'Welsh Gower' with Rhossili in 'English Gower'. Planned for completion in 2000 further branches and circular walks connected with the route will be involved.

Millennium Coastal Park Llanelli.
The new park stretches unbroken from the Loughor bridge, boundary between Carmarthenshire and Gower, to Pembrey Country Park and Cefn Sidan sands. A footpath and cycleway (part of the Celtic Trail) traverses it's length. There is a visitor centre at North Dock Llanelli.

St Illtyd's Walk.
A 64 mile route linking Pembrey Country Park with Margam Park, east of Swansea.

The Country Code

Enjoy the countryside and respect it's life and work.
Guard against all risk of fire.
Fasten all gates.
Keep your dogs under close control.
Keep to public paths across farmland.
Use gates and stiles to cross fences, hedges and walls.
Leave livestock, crops and machinery alone.
Take your litter home.
Help to keep all water clean.
Protect wildlife, plants and trees.
Take special care on county roads.
Make no unnecessary noise.

Worms Head

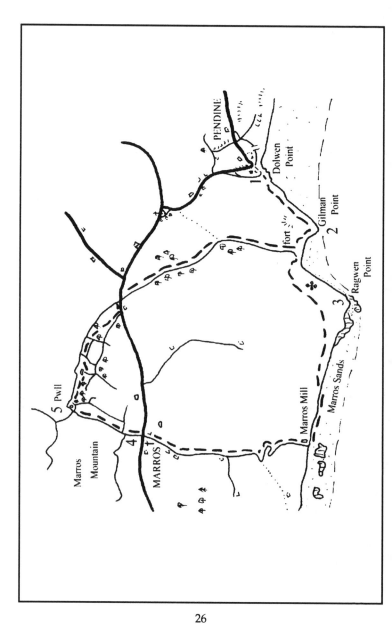

PENDINE

Dolwen Point

Gilman Point

fort

1

2

Ragwen Point

3

Marros Sands

Marros Mill

5 Pwll

Marros Mountain

4

MARROS

Pendine/Pentywyn – Gilman Point – Ragwen Point – Marros Sands – Marros – Pwll – Gilman Point – Pendine/Pentywyn

OS Maps:	1:50 000 Tenby 158; 1:25 000 000 Explorer 177 Carmarthen & Kidwelly, Pathfinder Pendine 1105 (SN 20/30).
Start:	Pendine. It is possible to start from Marros – parking on the side of the minor road, opposite the church.
Access:	Pendine is on the coastal road between Laugharne and Amroth, Pembrokeshire. Bus 351 Pendine – Amroth – Saundersfoot – Tenby operates Mondays to Saturdays. Bus 222 Pendine – Laaugharne – Carmarthen extends on Sundays to include Amroth, with connections to Tenby.
Parking:	Parking in Pendine or on Pendine Sands.
Grade:	Moderate – steep sections leading up to Gilman and Ragwen Points.

Points of Interest:

1. Nowadays Pendine is very much a holiday centre, offering a wide variety of water based activities, including safe bathing, and excellent accommodation and entertainment. It's sands run for some 5 miles to Laugharne Sands, with the sea running out for almost $1/2$ mile/$3/4$ kilometre at low tide. Most of the beach is controlled by the Ministry of Defence, who fire missiles out to sea; however Pendine is exempt from the danger area, as is the rest of the beach when red flags are not flying. The sands, along with those stretching on to Amroth and Saundersfoot in Pembrokeshire, were the scenes of rehearsals for the Normandy D-Day landings. Pendine church, dedicated to St Margaret, has a small 16th or 17th century tower with an unusual slate roof – the tower is the only original survivor from extensive rebuilding in 1869 apart from a 14th century seven sided font. There is in the grounds a cast iron headstone from 1888, set back against the wall and, almost opposite, a two tier preaching cross with the stem broken off. Further out from Pendine, on the road to Red Roses, is the originally 13th century church

Speed

Pendine has had a long and distinguished career in the history of land speed records. From 1924 to 1927 Malcolm Campbell and John Godfrey Parry Thomas contested with each other for ownership of the title the fastest man on earth. Land speed records date back to 1898 when the first clashes took place in France; an electrically powered car taking the initial record at 39.24 mph. Electric power achieved 65.79 mph until the monopoly was broken in 1902 by a steam powered car; the first petrol driven car taking the record for the first time in late 1902. The 100 mph barrier was broken in 1904. In 1914 the governing body defined the land speed record as the average of runs made once in opposite directions over a measured distance of a mile or a kilometre. The closed racing circuit of Brooklands had been used for land speed records but Pendine, for a few days a year, offered firm flat sand with room for a 2 mile run-up and a 2 mile run-down from the measured distance; one of the finest surfaces in Europe. In September 1924 Campbell raced *Bluebird* – all the Campbell family's cars are *Bluebirds*; the name derives from Maeterlinck's play *The Bluebird* – to a new record, and in July 1925 became the first man to crack the 150 mph barrier. Parry Thomas took the record from Campbell twice in 1926, but was killed in March 1927 when his car *Babs* overturned, becoming the land speed record's first, but not last, fatality. *Babs* was buried in the sands, though it has now been disinterred and restored. The same month saw the 200 mph record broken at Daytona Florida, Campbell regaining the record at Pendine in February 1928. However Pendine's sands were not suited for the increasingly higher speeds, and Daytona and Bonneville Salt Flats in Utah became favoured locations. Jet and rocket powered cars now dominate. The current record is held by Britain; in October 1997 at Black Rock Desert, Nevada, Andy Green, driving for Richard Noble in the Thrustcc, broke the sound barrier for the first time at Mach 1.002 i.e. a 2 way average of 763.035 mph. There now exist different classes for different powered vehicles. *Bluebird* returned to Pendine in 1998, this time in the shape of an electric *Bluebird*, with Don Wales, grandson to Sir Malcolm Campbell, at the wheel. In June 2000 he set a new British land speed record here of   128 mph. The current world record for electric vehicles is 245 mph – *Bluebird Electric* hope to take the record.

The land speed attempts were just the tip of the iceberg. Racing has always been part of Pendine's history, whether foot races, horse or machine, and with money prizes. *Pendine Races* in the early 20th century was very much an annual summer event, traditionally fitted in between the hay and corn harvest. Motor racing meant both car and bike, and the first 'official' bike race took place in 1905, with a prize of £3. The slipway was built to facilitate access to the shore. The races attracted huge crowds, star drivers and the best of local talent – the machine was new and speed was very much a futurist event. Air ace Amy Johnson dropped in during 1933 to see for herself, flying from Pendine on a transatlantic flight in the *Sea Farer*. The golden age, particularly for motor bikes, was the 1920s, and races continued to be held throughout the 1930s and 1940s, until the end came in 1955 when they could no longer pay their way. 1996 saw the opening of the *Museum of Speed*; a tribute to the Pendine record breakers and the *Pendine Races* – when not out on display, *Babs* is the prime exhibit. Nearby Pembrey Motor Racing Circuit offers current racing fare, with formula 3, vintage cars, bikes, truck races and rallying.

of Eglwyscymyn, also dedicated to St Margaret. There is a well worn ogham stone in the grounds, ogham being a 5th and 6th century Irish script cut into stones usually to mark the grave of aristocracy, and inside there are traces of 13th and 15th century murals. At one time there was also a chained Welsh language Bible, one of the editions from 1770, and an old pilgrim bottle.

2. Gilman Point, together with Telpyn Point at the western end of Marros Sands, is one of the principal seabird colony locations of Carmarthen Bay. Together with Wharley Point near Llansteffan these cliffs are virtually the only area of rocky coast in Carmarthenshire. The bay is of importance for the numbers of common scoter it supports; prior to the Sea Empress oil spill of 1996 the bay supported some 30% of the British population, but this large diving sea duck suffered badly in the wake of the spill. There is a large Iron Age fort here, with a massive curving ditch and bank on the northern side to add to the protection afforded by the cliffs. There is evidence of other defensive banks, as well as field walls and hut circles.

3. Clear days offer one of the finest views over Carmarthen Bay and beyond to Lundy Island and Devon. To the immediate left is Gilman Point, and beyond the flat sandy lands of Pendine and Laugharne Burrows backed by soft hills. Beyond is the Gower peninsula, with the Worms Head at it's prow. From the Worm it is 17 miles across the bay to Caldey Island (Ynys Bŷr) and the Pembrokeshire coast. The bay itself is a shallow sandy bay, wide open to the prevailing south westerlies. The area from Marros to the Pendine coast has been declared a Site of Special Scientific Interest (SSSI) for it's geological, botanical and marine biological interest. The sections of coal measures and millstone grit which dominate the bay from Tenby to Marros Sands give way to a belt of limestone, with it's cave indented cliffs hammered out by the sea. Beyond Gilman Point the limestone gives way to Old Red Sandstone and blown sand. Low tides reveal a submerged forest, lost thousands of years ago when the seas rose. The area has proved a skeleton coast for many ships – the outline of one can be seen buried in the sand close to the shore between Ragwen Point and Marros mill. There are four (possibly five) neolithic burial chambers dating from the 4th to the 3rd millennium BC here. They are to the left of the path as it begins it's

Marros Sands

descent to the sands, on a rocky level of jumbled stone, gorse and bracken close to the cliff edge. Identifying them is difficult, the jumble of slabs makes identification problematic; one upturned slab can look much like another. Even when built they would have been difficult to locate; quite possibly deliberately so. Their alignment·is north – south, facing Gilman Point. The coastline when they were built would have been quite different; the Burrows and the flat lands behind are of quite recent origin. It is possible that the chambers are of the passage grave type, if so this would make them the only examples of their kind in this part of Wales. Artefacts found during excavations in the early 20th century are housed in the National Museum of Wales at Cardiff.

4. Marros village lies close by Marros Mountain, on the main coastal road between Pendine and Amroth. The church, dedicated to St Lawrence, was originally 13th century to which a 14th century tower and porch have been added. As well as acting as a last line of defence in more troubled times and an important lookout for mariners traversing Carmarthen Bay and beyond, the tower also, at one time, housed the local school – the upper room has a fireplace for those slate-black winter days. However, since the closure of the tower doorway, entrance has been through a hole in the vault! The church was partly rebuilt in the early Victorian era. There is an ancient lichened cross by the porch. The unusual war memorial is in the style of a megalithic monument; a reference pointer to the neolithic burial chambers at Ragwen Point.

5. The wood, much coppiced, and like it's sister further along the route, has the aura of one of those magical woods that survive in hidden places away from the common. Once quarried, it's floor is now carpeted with wild garlic and bluebells, and is at it's finest and greenest from April to June.

Walk Directions: [-] denotes Point of Interest

1. Starting in Pendine [1] either walk past the Cliff Snack Bar, or ascend the steps from the beach, and follow the steps up Dolwen Point to join the cliff path leading to Gilman Point [2]. (Alternatively if the tide is well out walk along the sands to the beach lying between Gilman Point and Ragwen Point).

2. Once near Gilman Point bear left and down, away from the banks of the Iron Age fort, and join a wide path as it descends to the beach.

3. Once at the beach take the zig-zag path leading uphill, initially skirting a stern-looking wall, and continue up to Ragwen Point. There is a finger post at the beach marking the Carmarthen Bay Coastal Path.

4. From Ragwen Point [3] take the direction indicated by the finger post, downhill and left. The waymarked path continues downhill right. Continue ahead on the path, even where a more distinctive path crosses it, to reach Marros Sands.

5. Aim for the private house adjacent to the beach. Continue past it and the ruins of Marros mill, to cross a stream and almost immediately, at a finger post, turn right and go ahead on the path to reach the road leading to the private dwelling.

6. Continue uphill on the road to reach Marros.

7. From Marros [4] go ahead on the track leading across Marros Mountain towards *Honey Cottage*. Right of way is indicated by a metal walking man sign, next to the BT telephone box.

8. After 0.5 miles/0.75 kilometres where the main track bends left, continue on a smaller path leading off the track, and bearing right cross in front of Pwll house to reach a gate.

9. Continue ahead on the level path alongside the fence [5].

10. On leaving the wood, head for the obvious gap in the hedgebank opposite, ahead and slightly right. Once in this next field make for the lower field ahead left, and keep to it's right edge to enter a wood.

11. Continue on the path through the wood. Just before entering a field there is an impressive old limekiln on the left – best viewed from below.

12. Keep to the left of the field to join a track leading through the farm to the minor road.

13. At the minor road turn left. Once at the bottom of the dip in the road, and opposite an impressive entrance on the left, turn right onto a road and continue for over a mile/1.5 kilometres to reach the beach.

14. From the beach return to Pendine via Gilman Point.

Facilities

All available in Pendine. Museum of Speed at Pendine. Green Bridge Inn on coastal road between Marros and Pendine. BT telephone at Marros.

Laugharne – Sir John's Hill – Broadway –
The Laques – Laugharne Church – Delacorse – The
Boat House – Laugharne

OS Maps:	1:50 000 Tenby 158, Swansea & Gower 159: 1:25 000 Explorer 177 Carmarthen & Kidwelly, Pathfinder St Clears & Laugharne 1081 (SN 21/31) and Pendine 1105 (SN 20/30).
Start:	Car park below Laugharne Castle.
Access:	Laugharne is on the A4066 coastal road between St Clears and Pendine. Bus 222 from Carmarthen to Pendine operates daily, including Sunday.
Parking:	Car park below Laugharne Castle.
Grade:	Moderate.

Points of Interest:

1. Dylan Thomas, the town's most famous resident, described Laugharne as *this timeless, mild, beguiling island of a town . . . there is nowhere like it anywhere at all.* Laugharne has always been proud of it's independence, and it has the history to prove it. It was the successive male members of the de Brian family – conveniently, and as if to prove a point, all called Guy – who remodelled and strengthened the existing Norman castle from the late 12th to the late 14th centuries, and it was in 1291 that the town was granted it's charter, still in force today. One of the burgesses entitlements is shares in land at the Hugden, one of the very rare survivals of medieval strip fields in Britain – the walk passes along the foot of the Hugden; the strips are well preserved. Little now remains of the medieval town, though the original defence lines and the position of the town gates are roughly known. The name Laugharne derives from the welsh Lacharn, which predates the 13th century charter, this in itself appearing to be a corruption of Tal la Corran, the headland of the Corran, the river which flows through the town to meet the river Taf below the castle. This once tidal inlet has now been paved over to form the Grist – the name probably derives

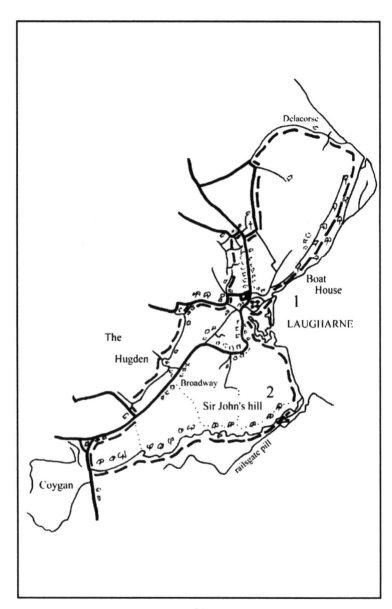

Delacorse

Boat
House

1

LAUGHARNE

The

Hugden

Broadway

2

Sir John's hill

railsgate pill

Coygan

from a grist mill that one stood here – the centre of the Grist is marked by the Celtic cross. The salt marsh and creeks which lean out seawards have only formed recently, over the last 100 years or so.

The castle itself has a mellow, attractive look and feel; built of local Old Red Sandstone with additions of attractive green stone by Guy de Brian VII in the mid 14th century Dylan Thomas found it in *Poem in October – as brown as owls*. After the death of Guy de Brian VII in 1390 the castle's fortunes declined, only to be revived in the late 16th century when it was granted by Elizabeth I to Sir John Perrot. With defence less a priority in Elizabethan times Perrot set about transforming the castle, as he did with his main residence at Carew in Pembrokeshire, into a luxurious Elizabethan mansion. With Perrot's arrest for treason the castle's fortunes once again declined. In the late 19th century, with the castle a Romantic ruin, the outer ward was laid out in a formal garden, and these, together with the castle, have been restored and are open during the summer months. Both Thomas and Richard Hughes, author of *A High Wind in Jamaica,* have found the castle's gazebo conducive to writing. Laugharne's church, dedicated to St Martin, dates from the late 14th century, with it's two porches and the majority of it's windows dating from the late 19th century. There is a fine disk headed 9th/10th century sculptured cross, now kept in the church for safekeeping.

Laugharne Castle

35

Dylan and Caitlin Thomas are buried in the churchyard, their graves marked by a simple white cross. There is a memorial plaque to Dylan Thomas in the church, a replica of the one at Poet's Corner in Westminster Abbey. Thomas first moved to Laugharne in May 1938, leaving for London in July 1940. He returned again in March 1949 when the town and the Boat House became his main home. The Boat House and the writing shed (Laugharne's first garage!) are now a heritage centre. Thomas' last major work, *Under Milk Wood*, was mostly written in Laugharne, (and often about Laugharne), and was first performed in the USA, some 6 months before his death.

2. Sir John's hill turns it's back on Laugharne to look out over the rivers of Taf and Tywi, and over Laugharne and Pendine Burrows, West Wales' largest spit and sand dune system. The system itself is recent, having begun to develop only since 1800; prior to this the coastline would have been marked by the present low line of hills, with Afon Taf being much wider. The coastline is now stable, and has been much used as marginal grazing land. That area not now used as a firing range by the Ministry of Defence, who have had access to the area since the trial Normandy landings took place here, is under the care of Carmarthenshire County Council. At the edge of Sir John's hill, and now demolished by quarrying, Coygan cave once stood, slung like a hunchback and looking out over a once cool and grassy plain that in prehistoric times was Carmarthen Bay. There would have been stands of birch and pine, with herds of mammoth, bison and reindeer. Before it's extinction the cave was excavated five times, the last in 1963. Most of the bones found were woolly rhinoceros, cave bear, Irish elk, bison, reindeer and hyena, and was most probably home to that master scavenger, the hyena. Stone tools found indicate human occupation at some stage by Neanderthal man, and have been dated to about 45,000 years before present. Later neolithic, and, possibly, mesolithic peoples found the site conducive to more permanent settlement. From the late 18th century until the early 20th the limestone quarried at Coygan was transported along a horse drawn tramway to waiting ships at Railsgate pill – lime was required as fertilizer and mortar; transport is now by road. On his return to Laugharne to live in 1949 Dylan Thomas wrote *Over Sir John's Hill* in celebration . . . *and a black cap of jackdaws Sir John's just hill dons, and again the gulled birds hare to the hawk on fire, the halter height, over Towy's fins . . .*

Walk Directions   [-] denotes Point of Interest

1. Starting from the car park walk along the foreshore away from Laugharne [1] along the metal track towards the pumping station. Note: this section can flood at high tides!

2. Just before the station and a bench take the waymarked path on the right leading up into woods and on to Sir John's hill.

3. Just over $1/2$ mile/$3/4$ kilometre, and by a viewpoint/notice board, choice of two paths. Take the left path and descend, passing another notice board, until the path levels [2].

4. Continue on the path, passing in front of Salt House farm and kennels (basset hounds), and continue on to reach the minor road and the quarry at Coygan.

5. Turn right, and again right at a 'No Through Road', to meet the main road. Continue ahead to reach Broadway Caravan and Camping Park. At the park take the minor road left, signposted Llansadurnon.

6. Almost immediately, opposite the entrance to the park, leave the minor road and cross a waymarked stile right, indicated by a walking man sign, and follow the path across the field – note the layout of the old strip fields of the Hugden!

7. Where the field path meets houses and a route to the main road, continue ahead by the edge of the field and take the clearly defined path on the right, leading off between trees.

8. Continue on the path, crossing a stone footbridge and, passing behind a house, join the track leading down to a minor road. Turn right.

9. Continue and take the next minor road on the left, opposite an old water pump and a sign for The Laques.

10. Continue ahead and take Holloway Road, which leads off ahead between houses.

11. Shortly join a path, and then cross two fields to meet a minor road – Horsepool Road. Turn right and at the main road cross to the church.

12. Walk passed the church and take the road immediately left, initially cobbled, marked 'Unsuitable for Wide Vehicles'. Continue ahead, uphill and then left. It is possible to join this road directly from the churchyard if preferred.

13. Continue to meet a T junction. Turn right and continue downhill to

Delacorse and the river. Continue across fields to join a woodland path.

14. Continue on the path, cross the road leading down to the shore, and continue directly ahead, passing Dylan Thomas's Boat House and his writing shed.

15. Just passed the shed, and opposite a whitewashed building and by the sign for the Boat House, turn left down steps to reach the paved walkway, leading below the castle and returning you to the starting point.

Facilities

Most available in Laugharne. Home from home for Dylan Thomas fans!

Llansteffan – Scott's Bay – Wharley Point – Lord's Park – Scott's Bay – St Anthony's Well – Parc Glas – Lanfach – Llansteffan

OS Maps:	1:50 000 Swansea & Gower 159: 1:25 000 Explorer 177 Carmarthen & Kidwelly, Pathfinder St Clears & Laugharne 1081 (SN 21/31) and Pendine 1105 (SN 20/30).
Start:	Llansteffan.
Access:	Llansteffan can be reached on the B4312 from Carmarthen (Caerfyrddin), or on minor roads via Llanybri. Bus 227 operates from Carmarthen (Caerfyrddin) daily, including Sunday.
Parking:	Beach car park at Llansteffan.
Grade:	Moderate.

Points of Interest:

1. Llansteffan's Georgian style makes it one of the most attractive villages in Carmarthenshire. Seemingly hidden away from the main arteries of communication, Llansteffan has looked to the river Tywi and the sea. Like it's neighbour Ferryside across the water, the village's popularity as a holiday destination began with the coming of the railway to Ferryside in 1852 – the local ferries would carry passengers across the river from the station. At one time a summer steamer called from Carmarthen (Caerfyrddin), on occasion steaming on to the West Country across the Bristol Channel. The mainly 13th/14th century church, built on an earlier 6th century site, is dedicated to the 6th century St Ystyffan, from whom the village takes it's name. Later 16th century additions include the Laques chapel. The round building in front of the church was once the village pound for housing stray cattle – it has been built up on the remaining walls!

Excavation on the castle site has shown that there was an earlier 6th century fort, with a double bank and ditch built across the neck to afford protection. Later 12th century Norman builders utilised these defences when a ringwork and bailey castle was established; made of

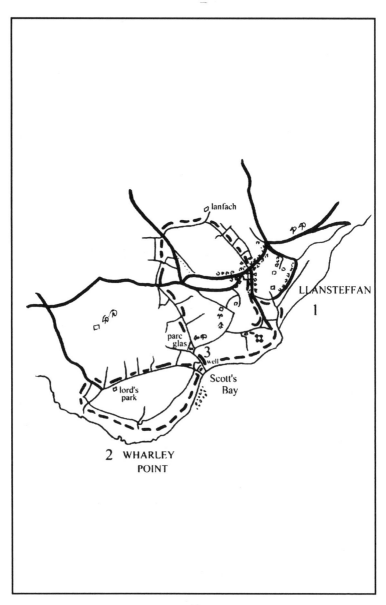

lanfach

LLANSTEFFAN

1

parc
glas

3

well

Scott's
Bay

lord's
park

2 WHARLEY
POINT

earth and timber it was vulnerable to constant attack and occupation by the Welsh princes. The first masonry structure dates from the late 12th/early 13th centuries, with the building of the inner curtain wall and wall walk, and the northern square gatehouse. Following capture during the campaign of Llywelyn Fawr in 1257, and subsequent recapture by the former lord de Camvilles, the castle was remodelled with two new D shaped towers and a double towered gatehouse. This Great Gatehouse offered both greater defence and the possibility of more comfortable accommodation for the lord – the fireplace on what was the second floor still preserves a contemporary carved female head, part of the decorative features. Later centuries saw the castle's decline in importance – during the Tudor era Henry VII conferred the castle on his uncle Jasper, who in those more settled times sought to make the castle more a place of habitation than a last line of defence. Turner painted the castle in 1795, contrasting the moonlit castle above with figures below tending the flames of a limekiln on shore. Entrance to the castle is free.

Llansteffan Castle

2. Wharley Point provides superb views over what are known colloquially as The Three Rivers. Most of Carmarthenshire's rivers flow south-west from the hills in the north east, with Afon Tywi the county's longest, flowing from the Cambrian mountains through Carmarthen (Caerfyrddin) and on passed Llansteffan to meet Afonydd Gwendraeth and Taf – Afon Taf by contrast with the other two flows through the agricultural lands to the west of Carmarthen (Caerfyrddin). During medieval times the three rivers would have been much wider, making the strategic importance of the three Norman castles at Laugharne, Llansteffan and Kidwelly more obvious than now. It was not until 1800 that the rivers began to assume their present shape. All three rivers are fished, with Afonydd Taf and Tywi both fished by coracle for salmon and sea trout – Afon Tywi is particularly well favoured. There is a well established heronry by Wharley Point, with the section between the point and the wood at Craig Ddu a Site of Special Scientific Interest (SSSI) – the area is particularly rich in maritime lichen flora.

3. The importance of St Anthony's well may date back to Celtic times when wells, rivers and trees were seen as objects of religious devotion. This particular well was adopted by a 6th century Christian hermit who called himself St Anthony after the 1st century St Anthony of Egypt. The 1st century St Anthony is regarded as the father of organised Christian monasticism, and his exotic visions and stoic endurance during his retreat in the Egyptian desert have made him a highly popular figure in Christian historiography, and in art and literature, right up to the 20th century. The 6th century St Anthony adopted the well and used the waters to baptise converts to the 'new' religion – he was to exercise much influence on the church in south Wales. The site was well chosen; with pilgrims for St David's crossing the river at Ferryside, and continuing on from Llansteffan to cross further round the headland across Afon Taf to Laugharne. The ruined church of St Michael, close by where Afon Cywyn flows into Afon Taf above Laugharne, is often known as the Pilgrim's church on account of the decorated late 12th or early 13th century gravestones in the churchyard – human figures depicted on the slabs have been thought to depict pilgrims, though they may be those of the Norman lords who once lived in the ruined motte and bailey castle nearby.

Walk Directions   [-] denotes Point of Interest

1. Starting from the car park [1] either walk along the beach or, if the

42

tide is in, along the sea wall to shortly reach a tarmac road leading down to the beach.

2. If the tide is out it is possible to walk along the sand to Scott's Bay; if not, or if preferred, turn right onto the road and then immediately left up stone steps and follow the cliff path on to Scott's Bay.

3. Continue ahead through white gates, cross the stone bridge, and continue on the path to Wharley Point [2].

4. Continue on the path as it leads inland to meet the minor road leading to Lord's Park.

5. Turn right and continue on the waymarked path through the farm and, keeping to the right edge, cross fields to meet a path leading back down to Scott's Bay.

6. Again cross the bridge and turn left on an inland path. A short distance on the left is a gate set into a brick wall with a slate plaque above left marked *Ffynnon Antwn Sant*. This gives access to St Anthony's well [3].

7. Continue on the path to shortly turn left and pass in front of Parc Glas (at one time Parc Glas, then known as Tafarn Llaeth [the Milk Inn], served up rum and milk!) to reach a stile. Turn right and continue uphill to the corner, cross a stile right into another field, and follow the left edge to reach a minor road.

8. Continue ahead across two fields to reach another minor road. Cross and continue ahead on the track to Lanfach – where the track bends left, continue ahead and then right across a stile.

9. Continue across fields, keeping to the right edge, to meet a path adjacent to a wall and leading down to Llansteffan.

10. Cross the road and continue on Church Road – once passed the houses there is a kissing gate on the left which gives access to the path leading down to the starting point – the road ahead will take you on to the castle.

Facilities

Most available in Llansteffan – public toilets and café/shop at the beach car park. It is not safe to bathe at Scott's Bay, where there is an emergency telephone.

1 FERRYSIDE

The Cliff

Ty Mawr

Broadlay

Tregoning Hill

2

St Ishmael's church

Pant

Pengay

Queen's

Tanylan farm

3 LLANSAINT

Ferryside – Tregoning Hill – St Ishmael's Church – Pengay Farm – Llansaint – Broadlay – Ferryside

OS Maps:	1:50 000 Swansea & Gower 159: 1:25 000 Explorer 177 Carmarthen & Kidwelly, Pathfinder St Clears & Laugharne 1081 (SN 21/31) and Pendine 1105 (SN 20/30).
Start:	Ferryside.
Access:	Ferryside is on the main train line between Carmarthen (Caerfyrddin), Llanelli and Swansea (Abertawe). Bus 198 from Carmarthen (Caerfyrddin) to Llanelli stops at Ferryside and Llansaint all days including Sundays. Parking site at Ferryside in centre of village.
Parking:	Moderate.
Grade:	

Points of Interest:

1. Ferryside (Glanyferi), as the name implies, grew up around the ferry which operated for centuries, ferrying passengers and pilgrims across the river to Llansteffan and vice versa. The last ferries ceased in 1948. Brunel drove his Great Western Railway through Ferryside, *en route* from Llanelli to Carmarthen (Caerfyrddin). Opening in 1852 the track was first laid on shingle to Brunel's own gauge, with sea defences to protect it from incoming tides – later it was elevated to the safety of an embankment, effectively cutting off the village from the shore. The railway boosted the holiday trade, with miners from the Rhondda mixing with Swindon railway workers and day trippers from Carmarthen (Caerfyrddin), Llanelli and Swansea (Abertawe). The railway gave work to many, but the sea has been the main supplier for employment. Afon Tywi is noted for it's sewin, and together with Llansaint the village has had a long history of cockling – at one time some 20-30 donkeys would be seen making their way up from the beach to the station, laden with cockles. Given it's proximity to the sea meant it was an ideal location for a lifeboat. The first in the area was the *Carmarthen Bay*, operating in the early 19th century either from Ferryside or Laugharne, and which remained in service until damaged

in 1843. The next boat arrived in the January of 1860, and this time a boat house was specially built for it at Ferryside. The first motorised lifeboat dates from 1948, with the *Caroline Oats Avers and William Maine*, arriving from St Ives, the last to flourish; the station finally closing in 1960. It is now home to the flourishing River Towy Yacht Club. The memorial plaque by the entrance lists lives saved, and makes for interesting reading. Traditionally the village is split into two parts – the Cliff a residential area built above the Village down below.

2.   The church here is dedicated to St Ishmael, a nephew to St David, and who is credited with setting up the first structure in the 6th century. The present building dates back to the 13th century, with possible 14th century additions – the windows are mid 19th century. The porch, topped by a sundial, continues up as a saddle back tower, and gives the building a fine flourish. It is the main parish church. On the foreshore below, at low tides, are the remains of a lost village which once lay snug at the foot of the church – the village was probably lost in the storms of the early to mid 17th century. A similar storm in 1869

St Ishmael's Church

46

lay bare some walls reaching up to two feet in height, but now it is mostly buried beneath the dunes by the railway line.

3. Llansaint is an attractive hilltop village, it's streets clustered around it's church; it has been designated a conservation area, and traces of the old medieval strip fields still surround the village. The church site is possibly Iron Age, with the first church possibly 5th century. The present church incorporates two 5th or 6th century memorial stones to probably local Irish chieftains – Vennisetl and Cimesetl. They are located towards the bottom of the church wall by the small lean-to building facing towards the entrance path. Llansaint has always been noted for it's cockle women; they were the mainstay of the cockle trade, though there were others from Ferryside and Kidwelly. Prior to 1900 an annual total of almost six hundred and fifty tons made their way out by rail from Ferryside for sale in the market place.

Walk Directions   [-] denotes Point of Interest

1. Starting from Ferryside [1] take the road between the Ship Inn and White Lion hotel and continue on a level and wooded track marked by a 'Cycles Prohibited' sign.

2. Stay on the level to finally meet a minor road. Turn right, and then shortly left to join the Llansaint and Kidwelly road.

3. After a short distance, and immediately after the drive walls of a house, ascend up steep steps and continue to reach a stile giving access to a field.

4. Turn right (not ahead as indicated by the waymark) and follow the path along the hedge, and cross a stile to a sometimes muddy path, and then head diagonally right across an open field to meet a stile in the top right corner.

5. Cross the stile to join a path which shortly joins a wider more open path. Turn left and continue on the path along National Trust owned Tregoning hill – superb views over the estuary and the distant Preseli hills in Pembrokeshire – to rejoin the minor road to Llansaint and Kidwelly. The Tregoning family, originally from Cornwall, made their wealth from their tinplate works at Llanelli.

6. Continue along the road, passing St Ishmael's church [2] until 'Gwelfro' is reached. Take the 'No Through Road' on the left, and continue uphill to Pengay farm. (If the short section onwards from Pant

is overgrown, as it can be in high summer, it is an easy matter to continue on the coastal road to Tanylan farm (Carmarthen Bay Touring and Camping Site) – there is an interesting and well populated duck pond on the right here – and to turn left on to the road up to Llansaint, and then again to turn left to pass Queen's to reach the footpath leading up on the right to Llansaint).

7.   Continue on the road through Pengay farm – there is a splendid bell from a Dutch shipwreck in 1760 hanging above an arched gateway on the left – and after a short distance turn right and cross a stile by a farm gate. Great views of Pen-bre (Pembrey) and Gŵyr (Gower) ahead.

8. Follow the right hedge to a stile and continue on a waymarked zig zag path through wood to reach a minor road.

9. Turn left and almost immediately cross a stile and ascend diagonally right on a path to a stile. Continue alongside the hedge to reach buildings and continue on to meet a minor road.

10. Turn left and continue uphill to Llansaint [3].

11. From Llansaint take the Ferryside and Kidwelly road, and just before the Joiners Arms and Sion Calvinistic Methodist chapel take the gated path on the left indicated by a green walking man.

12. Continue down the lane to a gate and stile. Cross and continue diagonally right to a metal stile. Continue, keeping to the left of the fence of the treatment works below, to reach a minor road.

13. Directly opposite the gates of the treatment works is a footbridge

across the stream – ascend left through wood to meet a stile giving access to a field. Continue uphill keeping to the left edge to cross a stone stile onto the minor road from Pengay farm.

14. Turn right and continue on the road until, where the road turns sharp right, bear left across a stile and continue across waymarked fields to reach a green lane descending between fields to the minor road at Broadway.

15. Turn right and continue on the road to shortly turn left at Tŷ Mawr (second on the left, just past the entrance to Plas farm), and follow the lane right in front of houses to reach a gate at the end of the lane giving access to a field.

16. Bear left and keep to the left edge to reach a gate. Once in the second field bear diagonally right to cross a stile onto a minor road.

17. Bear left and continue on the road back to Ferryside and the starting point – the route is known as the Portway, and is the ancient track down to the ferry.

Facilities

Most available in Ferryside. Good pub, the Kings Arms, in Llansaint.

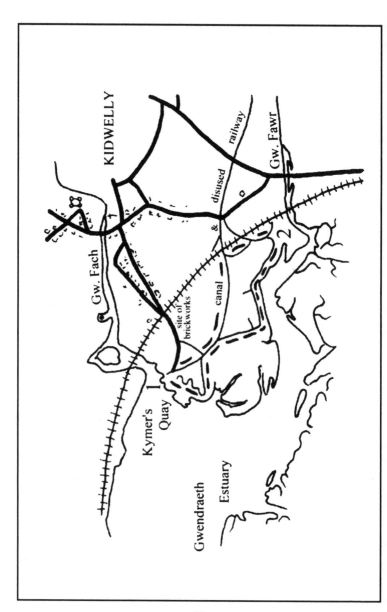

Cydweli/Kidwelly (Kymers) Quay Circular

OS Maps: 1:50 000 Swansea & Gower 159; 1:25 000 Explorer 177
                Carmarthen & Kidwelly, Pendine 1105 (SN 20/30),
                Llanelli (North) 1106 (SN 40/50).
Start: Car park/picnic site at Kidwelly Quay.
Access: Kidwelly Quay is reached from the main road through
                Kidwelly, and is approximately 1 mile/1.5 kilometres
                from the castle. Turn onto the minor road signposted
                Station which will lead to the Quay, crossing the rail line
                en route. Kidwelly is on the main bus and train routes
                from Carmarthen (Caerfyrddin) to Llanelli and Swansea
                (Abertawe).
Parking: Kidwelly Quay.
Grade: Easy.

Points of Interest:

1. Kidwelly is situated at the junction of Afon Gwendraeth Fach and
Afon Gwendraeth Fawr, which meet together below the town to form
the Gwendraeth estuary. The northern river, Gwendraeth Fach,
descends through fertile valleys, whilst the southern river makes it's
way through the once industrialised edge of the South Wales coalfield.
When the Normans built their castle the sea would have been much
further inland than now; there has been a constant battle between man
and sea over ownership of the land, with reclamation a constant theme
from the Middle Ages until well into the 19th century. It was the
building of the A484 and the railway in the early 1850s that effectively
completed reclamation. Constructed partly on a causeway they sealed
off the marsh which once stretched from Kidwelly down to Pen-bre
(Pembrey).

   With access to the sea, medieval Kidwelly port rivalled that of
Carmarthen (Caerfyrddin) as the busiest in South Wales, with imports
of iron, brass and domestic goods, and a booming trade in wool and
textiles from the textile mills on Afon Gwendraeth Fach. However
silting has always been Kidwelly's problem, and the silting of the

estuary in the 16th century reduced the town's importance as a port. The advent of industrialisation in the 18th century helped restore fortunes, with new wharves and shipyards being established. To offset the difficulties of navigation on Afon Gwendraeth Fawr Thomas Kymer, a Pembrokeshire man and one of the leading local industrialists, built a canal here from 1766-68 to transport anthracite and culm from his coal pits and levels at nearby Pwll Y Llygod and Carway to the quay for loading. 3 miles/4.75 kilometres long the canal was the first commercial canal of substance in South Wales. Orders were received from Ireland, North Wales, England and the Continent. However silting in the estuary once again raised it's ugly head, and with the exhaustion of coal reserves the port declined once more. Most of Kymer's canal became part of the Kidwelly and Llanelli canal, and then, as part of the Burry Port and Gwendraeth Valley Railway, lines were laid along the towpath. Continual silting of the estuary occasioned the loss of the quay's importance, and accordingly this section of the line to the junction at nearby Tycoch was closed in 1929, with the lines being raised in 1933. The area is nowadays a Special Area of Conservation; the mud flats provide good feeding for overwintering waders and wildfowl. The estuary itself runs out for close on 7

Gwendraeth Fawr

miles/11 kilometres to join Afonydd Taf and Tywi in a common estuary.

2. The embankment here is a 19th century sea wall, part of the continuous fight to keep the sea at bay. The modern passenger railway line was inaugurated in 1852, Brunel and other guests of the South Wales Railway travelling the line from Swansea (Abertawe) to Carmarthen (Caerfyrddin). Just south of the line, adjacent to the access road to the quay, was the site of Stephen's Kidwelly Brickworks. Stephen's already had probable control of a smaller brickworks by the station in the early 1890s, and chose the new site for expansion in 1903. Using silica and lime from his quarry workings on nearby Mynydd-y-Garreg, Stephen's & Co was one of three *dinas* silica brickworks in the vicinity – *dinas* was used as a particular term for a firebrick, useful for lining furnaces. The brickworks closed in 1965, and the site is now cleared.

Walk Directions   [-] denotes Point of Interest

1. The walk begins [1] at the picnic site, and after crossing a footbridge follows the edge of the field/estuary boundary until the path mounts an embankment facing Afon Gwendraeth Fawr and turns inland [2].

2. Keeping the railway line on the right continue on paths through fields, until Thomas Kymer's 18th century canal is reached. Follow the canal back to the staring point.

Facilities

All facilities available in Kidwelly.

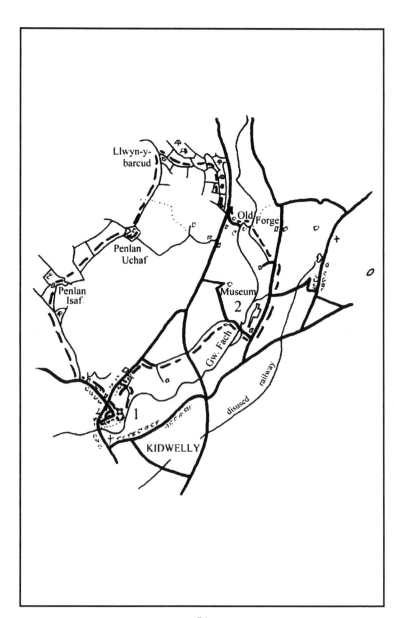

Llwyn-y-barcud

Old Forge

Penlan Uchaf

Penlan Isaf

Museum

2

Gw. Fach

disused railway

1

KIDWELLY

Kidwelly – Penlan Isaf – Penlan Uchaf – Llwyn-y-barcud – Old Forge – Kidwelly Industrial Museum – Kidwelly

OS Maps:	1:50 000 Swansea & Gower 159; 1:25 000 Explorer 177 Carmarthen & Kidwelly, Llanelli (North) 1106 (SN 40/50).
Start:	Kidwelly Castle.
Access:	Kidwelly is on the main bus and train routes between Carmarthen (Caerfyrddin), Llanelli and Swansea (Abertawe).
Parking:	Car park by Kidwelly Castle. The castle is well signposted.
Grade:	Moderate.

Points of Interest:

1. Kidwelly's early history is vague; it is known that pilgrims visited the area, and there were chapels dedicated to the 6th century saints Cadog and Teilo. There is also an association, noted in place names, with the early Christian king Cunedda Wledig. Norman power began in 1106 when Henry I granted the commote of Cydweli to Roger, Bishop of Salisbury. He constructed the first timber castle, and founded a small priory, now vanished. The weakness of it's materials left the new castle vulnerable to Welsh territorial repossession, and in the mid 13th century Pain de Chaworth began rebuilding in stone. The castle was built in the new concentric style, a response to the growing power of the Welsh nationalism of Llywelyn the Great. The castle had two lines of defence; an inner ward with four round towers and portcullis gates set within a protected outer ward. The outer curtain wall and towers date from the early 14th century, and work on the Great Gatehouse, designed to withstand siege on it's own if necessary, was similarly begun. The gatehouse took nearly a century to complete, and was still unfinished when Owain Glyndŵr unsuccessfully attacked the castle in 1403. The Norman town was founded shortly after the castle, and of the once walled town only the early 14th century South Gate

remains, opposite the castle. By the early 1600s the castle was partly in ruins, with timber and lead stripped for recycling. The castle has two notable connections with the art world; circa 1480 the Dutch master Hans Memling painted, on commission from the castle's constable Sir John Dwnn, the *Dwnn Triptych* (National Gallery, London), which gives the oldest surviving portrait of a Welsh family, with a possible representation of the gatehouse in the background. The peripatetic Turner was here in 1795, drawing the castle from two different angles. His watercolour of 1832 of the castle, completed for *Picturesque Views in England and Wales*, is one of his finest.

Kidwelly in the Middle Ages was a busy and bustling place. In size in the mid 16th century it boasted a population of over a thousand inhabitants, making it one of the most sizeable towns in Wales – Swansea (Abertawe) and Cardiff (Caerdydd) both had similar populations. Nearby Carmarthen (Caerfyrddin), with two thousand inhabitants, was by repute the largest town in Wales. The church dates from the 14th century; it is believed that the priory was nearby. The porch-tower and spire were added circa 1400 – the addition of the clock has made this the town clock. There is in the church a 14th century alabaster figure of the Madonna; the church is dedicated to St Mary. One late 19th century vicar, incensed by the local women curtseying to the effigy, threw it out, only to be forced to re-house it! Another feature

Kidwelly Castle and Church

of interest is the fleur de lys to be found in a moulded panel. The emblem was that of the Virgin, and was also linked to the Arms of France and to the Flemings who are known to have settled in the wake of the Normans here as in neighbouring Pembrokeshire – they were noted experts in wool manufacture and dyeing. There is a splendid tower door ' . . . *the gateway of heaven'*, dating from 1713. The church was restored in 1884.

2. With the advent of industrialisation much of the later history of Kidwelly became tied up with the fortunes of coal and tinplate, with limestone and silica quarried from the limestone ridge of nearby Mynydd-y-Garreg, with the *dinas* silica brickworks in the area, and with initially the canals built to transport mineral wealth, and later with the railways built on or alongside the then obsolete canals. The town and borough council involved itself in many local concerns, including ownership of lime and silica quarries on Mynydd-y-Garreg, however not always to industrialists' satisfaction. Here, on the site of the present museum, a Dr John Lane of Bristol set up a stamping mill in 1721 to crush ore – he had been granted a licence by Kidwelly corporation in 1717 to search for copper and other minerals on Mynydd-y-Garreg. However by 1726 he was bankrupt. In 1737 Charles Gwynn of Kidwelly was given licence to build rolling and tin mills on the site, and from then on until 1941 there was a tinplate works on the site. It's history was nothing if not chequered, run by a series of partnerships, and with it's future uncertain. The early 1890s was a particularly trying period – up until 1891, when the US imposed a tariff on imports of tinplate, threequarters of Britains's tinplate, most of it from South Wales, was exported to that country. The tariffs were followed by slump, followed by the emigration of thousands of skilled Welsh tinplate workers to the USA, a state of affairs that the US planners had been expecting.

In 1864 and 1865 respectively, and as part of the Carmarthen and Cardigan Railway, a *lime line* was authorised by Parliament to be built from Kidwelly by way of Mynydd-y-Garreg to a point further north, and a *coal line* by way of Carway to Pontyberem. In 1866 Royal assent was given to the Gwendraeth Valleys Railway (GVR) to administer the new lines. Eventually in 1872, and as a standard gauge railway, track was laid to the quarries and limekilns at Mynydd-y-Garreg, but not beyond, and the *coal line* proposals were abandoned. In 1880 a connection was made with the tinplate works, and in 1904 the tinplate company took over running of the railway. Continuing difficulties in the industry led the Kidwelly works to seek amalgamation with other local Carmarthenshire tinplate companies in 1939, however by July 1941 Kidwelly was forced to close. In January 1948 the GVR became part of British Rail, but in 1960 the line to Mynydd-y-Garreg was declared formally closed. Following a period as a supply and stores depot the site became a museum, opening in 1987. *Margaret*, the main loco in use at the tinplates, formerly in use for the Maenclochog Railway in Pembrokeshire, has found her way (with help) to Scolton Manor Museum near Haverfordwest in Pembrokeshire. In it's heyday the tinplate company had been one of many scattered throughout the western part of the South Wales coalfield. With the building of the largest steelworks in Britain at Margam in 1951, and a linked tinplate works opening at Trostre, Llanelli in 1953 and at Felindre, Swansea in 1956, the heyday of the smaller tinplate companies was over.

Walk Directions   [-] denotes Point of Interest

1. Starting from the castle car park [1], walk up Castle Street, cross the main road through town, and go up Heol Y Feri (Ferry Road). It is signposted Ferryside and Llansaint.

2. Take the second turning right, walk up the road and join a wooded path. Public footpath sign at road.

3. After a short distance take the path leading left across the stream. A stone pillar marks the turning – the path ahead peters out by a field boundary.

4. Follow the path and farm track to Penlan Isaf, bearing right through the farm to reach a field stile on the left. Route clearly waymarked through farm. Good views of the Gwendraeth estuary, Pen-bre (Pembrey) forest and Gŵyr (Gower) from the track as you near the farm.

5. Cross the field diagonally right to a stile by a telegraph pole. Cross the stile and continue along the right edge of two fields. At the top right end of the second field cross two stiles right to Penlan Uchaf.

6. Bear left and where the farm track leads right to the main road continue ahead through the farmyard to reach a stile giving access to a green lane.

7. Continue on the green lane to shortly reach a crossroads of

footpaths. Continue ahead. The yellow waymarked man on the stile on the right looks a little as if he had been impaled there!

8.   After a short distance the lane joins a wider farm track – bear left until the track to Llwyn y barcud is reached, leading off to the right. There is a four way signpost here.

9.   Continue to Llwyn y barcud, using the two stiles that skirt the property. Continue ahead on a green lane to reach a stile on the left giving access to a field. Bear right – not ahead as is suggested by the yellow waymark – and keep to the right hand hedge of the field to enter a second field.

10. Aim for the gap in the hedge below and enter a third field. Keep to the right edge of this field, away from the hedge adjacent to the wood below, and where the field narrows continue bearing along the right edge on a path leading through brambles to reach a stile giving access to King's wood.

11. After a short distance join a wider path. Continue ahead on the level track, crossing two fields to reach a stile giving access to another track. Turn left to reach the main road. There are excellent views from the second field of the ridge of Mynydd-y-Garreg opposite, and of the river below, with to the right the outline of Gŵyr (Gower). The ornate (red-brick) building to the left of the village of Mynyddygarreg is a chapel.

12. Turn left and then right to join the road bearing sharp right. Follow the road downhill and cross Afon Gwendraeth Fach by a bridge and take the path bearing right behind the Old Forge.

13. Continue on the path to join a farm track. Bear left, and then right onto a minor road. Continue on the minor road to bear right by the Gwenllian Court hotel – Gwenllian was a Welsh princess who attacked the Norman's stronghold at Kidwelly in 1135; the battlefield is nearby. The Kidwelly Industrial Museum is adjacent to the hotel [2].

14. Follow the road as it bears left, and where it turns sharp right continue straight ahead on a green lane – still known today as Tinworks Lane. Continue, crossing the main A484 *en route*, to reach a track. Bear right to shortly join the main road through Kidwelly.

15. Turn left at the main road, and shortly bear left onto a tarmac road; sign showing 'Caution – Speedramps' here. Go ahead, passing the play area on your left, to join a path through a kissing gate. Sign marked

Llwybr Cyhoeddus (Public Footpath).

16. Follow the path as it skirts the Gwendraeth Fach, with the castle above. Just before a footbridge bear uphill right on a path to return to the starting point. The path ahead, across the footbridge, will take you into town, passing an antiques shop on the way .

Facilities

> All available in Kidwelly. The Industrial museum opens on the Easter weekend and from the May bank holiday to the August bank holiday. There is a short footpath around the old quarry of Mynydd-y-Garreg; accessible from the minor road from Kidwelly to Four Roads. A small lake has formed in the old workings. Great views over Carmarthen Bay on clear days.

Penybedd Wood – Penybedd – Ffrwd Fen – Coed – Coed Rhyal – Pen-bre/Pembrey – Penybedd Wood

OS Maps: 1:50 000 Swansea & Gower 159; 1:25 000 Explorer 177
             Carmarthen & Kidwelly, Explorer 10 Gower, Llanelli
             (North) 1106 (SN 40/50).
Start: Forest picnic site.
Access: From Pen-bre (Pembrey) follow the road signposted to
             Pembrey Country Park. The picnic site is on the right just
             past the railway bridge. Pen-bre (Pembrey) is on the
             main bus and train routes from Carmarthen
             (Caerfyrddin) to Llanelli and Swansea (Abertawe). Pen-
             bre (Pembrey) airfield is close by!
Parking: Car park at picnic site.
Grade: Moderate – woodland and field paths, some road
             walking.

Points of Interest:

1. Pembrey is a corruption of the Welsh name for the village, Pen-bre,
meaning 'end of the hill'. During the Iron Age there were two forts on
Pen-bre (Pembrey) mountain; the oldest, Carreg Lwyd, was in use from
400BC to 100AD, whilst Court Wood probably continued in occupation
until much later – there have been finds of second century Roman
pottery on site. Access to the forts is possible from the main road
through Pen-bre (Pembrey), Carreg Lwyd the most accessible. The hill
may also have been occupied during the Bronze Age. Following the
Norman conquest Pen-bre (Pembrey) became part of the Marches of
Wales, specifically a manor within the lordship of Kidwelly. The church
was certainly in existence by 1120, however the present building is
mostly 13th/14th century, and is dedicated to St Illtud. There is in the
grounds a memorial to those who have died in shipwrecks on Cefn
Sidan sands. One was Adeline Coquelin, niece of Josephine, consort of
Napoleon, who perished on *La Jeune Emma* in 1828.

The present coastline, stretching from Pen-bre (Pembrey) to
Pendine (Pentywyn), is of comparatively recent origin. Most of the

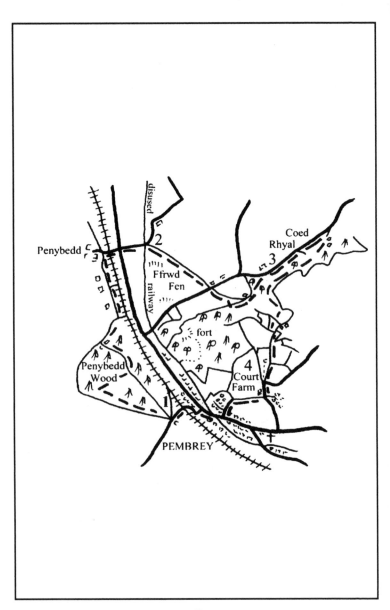

Penybedd

disused

2

Coed
Rhyal

3

Ffrwd
Fen

railway

fort

4
Court
Farm

Penybedd
Wood

1

PEMBREY

dunes have formed since medieval times, many only over the last 50 years. Some 5000/6000 years ago the sea would have been lapping at the foot of Pen-bre (Pembrey) mountain. There has been much land reclamation over the centuries, with drainage dykes and sea wall building continuing from the Middle Ages up until the early 19th century. The sands of the silken bank of Cefn Sidan are also of recent origin; it was there in outline only by 1800. 20th century initiatives have been dune stabilisation and the creation of Pen-bre (Pembrey) forest. Penybedd wood, where the walk begins, was formerly a nursery for Pen-bre (Pembrey) forest. During the 1930s some thirty local women were employed in growing trees from seed for planting on the already established dunes. The wood is part of Pen-bre (Pembrey) forest, and is managed as a Forest Nature Reserve.

Nearby Pembrey Country Park was itself created as a result of land reclamation in the late 1970s/early 1980s. Formerly the park was the site of a Royal Ordnance factory. At it's peak during World War II, some three thousand people were employed, production finally ceasing in 1965. The park, one of Wales' top spots, offers a variety of activities, with Cefn Sidan's 8 miles/13 kilometres of sands being one of the finest in Europe, with European Blue Flag status. There is still a military presence in the area, with fighter jets attacking aerial targets at the northern end of Pen-bre (Pembrey) forest – the targets are attacked from the landward side. One exciting new initiative is the transformation of the coastal area between Pen-bre (Pembrey) and Llanelli from one of industrial dereliction to the Millennium Coastal Park Llanelli, a 14 mile/22 kilometre coastal environmental project. Features, including a floating harbour, indoor arena and a watersports centre, are linked by a continuous footpath and cycleway.

2. A Site of Special Scientific Interest (SSSI), Ffrwd Fen, one of the few surviving areas of freshwater marsh in the locality, is in the care of the Wildlife Trust West Wales (WTWW). The rare habitats of wet grassland, fen and reed-bed allow specialist species to survive in an area where, in the early 1800s, a large marsh had spread from Kidwelly to Pen-bre (Pembrey). One of the now rare species that survive in wetland habitats like Ffrwd Fen is the water vole, whose lifestyle has recently been the subject of an interpretative land sculpture, mainly for children, at the nearby wetlands reserve of Penclacwydd. There is no access to Ffrwd Fen. The walk follows the north-eastern side of the reserve and accompanies the old Ashburnum canal, abandoned in 1818. From the

1670s to the 1920s the Ashburnum's were among the leading landowners and industrialists in the area; in 1796 the second Lord Ashburnum began construction on a $1^1/2$ mile/2.5 kilometre long canal reaching from below Coed Farm to Afon Gwendraeth Fawr at Pill Towyn. To exploit the seams of coal on his land the first Earl had used pack horses to transport the black gold from nearby Coed Rhyal and Coed y Marchog to ships on the Gwendraeth estuary and the Burry Inlet. The canal, inspired by nearby Kymer's canal at Kidwelly, replaced the horses, but by 1818 the coal was virtually exhausted.

A new harbour was built at Pen-bre (Pembrey) in 1819 to exploit resources from elsewhere in the locality. To connect the harbour with the Kidwelly and Llanelli canal at Pinged marsh, a tramroad and the 2 mile/3 kilometre Pembrey canal were completed by 1824. The new harbour failed to cope with the level of coal for shipment and in 1832 a new harbour was opened at Burry Port, with an extension to the Kidwelly and Llanelli canal completed by 1837. The Kidwellly and Llanelli canal was by far the most important in the area. 11 miles/17.5 kilometres long in it's final form, connecting Kidwelly, Cwm-mawr and Pont-iets with Burry Port, the Canal company was forced by competition from the railways to tranform itself by amalgamating with Burry Port Harbour Company in 1866, and becoming the Burry Port and Gwendraeth Valley Railway. The rail lines were built mostly on the canal bed, though occcasionally the towpath was used. Like the canal the old railway is now disused, though traces of both remain; tracks can be seen embedded in the tarmac road by the entrance to Ffrwd Fen. Burry Port is now the main harbour for Carmarthen Bay, with forty or more boats, many occupied in mostly part-time fishing for bass, or the odd one or two in tangle netting for lobster.

3. Coed Rhyal is, like Ffrwd Fen, managed by the Wildlife Trust West Wales. The wood comprises some 14 acres of sessile oak, much of it coppice re-growth. The wood overlies the coal measures which were exploited by Lord Ashburnum, and there are still open mine-shafts within the woodland; one prominent shaft is fenced off adjacent to the path.

4. Though now ruinous, Court farm has a long history. The earliest known family in the Norman manor of Pembrey were the 14th century Butlers of Court farm, and while the present building is not of that period it is the largest surviving Elizabethan building in the county of Carmarthen (Caerfyrddin).

Cwrt

Walk Directions [-] denotes Point of Interest

1. **[1]**. From the car park take the path to the left of the woodland. Continue on the path for $^1/_2$ mile/0.75 kilometres to reach a T junction. Turn right onto a wider path and continue to reach a crossroads. Turn left onto the main forestry track.

2. Continue past the forest office and continue along a permissive path/track to reach the crossroads at Penybedd.

3. Turn right, cross the railway line and the main road, and go up the minor road. After a short distance cross the old 19th century railway line and turn right onto the path leading through Ffrwd Fen nature reserve **[2]**. Signposts here marked Llwybr St Illtud and Mountain Walks.

4. Continue through the reserve to reach a minor road. Cross the road and continue up the track ahead. Do not go all the way to the house but turn right on a grassy path just before the track bends left. Cross the small open field and enter the wood. Sign Llwybr St Illtud Walk.

5. Turn left. Continue on the woodland path to reach a T junction. Turn left and descend to a minor road. Good panoramic views ahead, with the flat landscape backed on the left by Pen-bre (Pembrey) forest, with directly ahead the Gwendraeth rivers and, perched at the bottom of a ridge, Kidwelly with it's Norman castle.

6. Turn right. After a short distance there is a path going up steps on the right into woodland – ignore this, unless you require a short cut through Coed Rhyal! Parking area in front.

7. Continue along the road for $1/4$ mile/0.5 kilometres to join a track bending back right from the road. Signpost with walking man here. Cross the stile and almost immediately turn right onto a grassy path leading to Coed Rhyal [3]. Sign here indicating Mountain Walks.

8. Continue on the woodland path for $1/2$ mile/0.75 kilometres to cross a stile into an open field. Turn left and keeping to the left edge continue to the corner of the field where it bends left. Turn right and cross the field to a stile opposite leading into a smaller field.

9. Cross this field, cross another stile and turn and continue right. As you top the rise views open up of Penrhyn Gŵyr (the Gower peninsula). Continue along the right edge and descend through field/scrub to reach a road.

10. Continue a short distance on the road until just opposite 'Ar-y-bryn' road turn right onto a path leading past Cwrt's Elizabethan splendour [4].

11. Continue on the path to reach the main A484 through Pen-bre (Pembrey). Turn right, cross the road, and bear left onto the road leading to the Country Park and the starting point.

Facilities

All facilities available in Pen-bre (Pembrey) and neighbouring Burry Port. Local attractions include Pembrey Country Park and the Millennium Coastal Park Llanelli. There is also the Welsh Motor Sports Pembrey Circuit (once a Spitfire airfield) just north of the Country Park offering two and four wheeled entertainment – including formula 3, classic and vintage car races. Near Llanelli is Penclacwydd Wildfowl and Wetlands Centre, well worth a visit.

Llanmadoc – Llangenydd (Llangennith) – The Bulwark – Llanmadoc

OS Maps:	1:50 000 Swansea & Gower 159; 1:25 000 Explorer 10 Gower.
Start:	Llanmadoc. Can also start from Llangenydd if preferred.
Access:	Llanmadoc is easily accessible on minor roads leading to the north-western corner of Gower. Bus 16 from Swansea (Abertawe) to Llanmadoc and Llangenydd (not Sundays).
Parking:	In the centre of Llanmadoc.
Grade:	Moderate.

Points of Interest:

1. Llanmadoc takes it's name from it's founding as a religious settlement dedicated to the 6th century St Madoc. Madoc is believed to have been an Irish pupil of St David, who later became the first Bishop of Ferns in Ireland. Llanmadoc is the earliest Gower site for which there is firm Christian evidence. In the window sill of the south wall of the church is set what remains of a late 5th/early 6th century Latin inscribed Christian memorial stone to Vectus or Advectus, son of Guanus. There are also two inscribed pillar stones dating from the 7th/9th centuries in the nave. With the defeat of the last native ruler of Gŵyr (Gower) in 1106, the commote was acquired by the Norman, Henry, Earl of Warwick. In 1156 his wife Margaret, following Henry's death, granted the manor and church to the military order of the Knights Templar. Loss of territories in the Holy Land for the order to defend, and resentment of their enormous wealth and power in Europe, lead to the order's suppression by Pope Clement V in 1312. Their properties were ordered transferred to the Knights Hospitallers. Though Kings, notably French and English ones, often stepped in to take the lands and wealth for themselves, property here was transferred and added to the Hospitallers possessions already held in the neighbouring fee (or manor) of Llandimore. In 1540 their order was suppressed, and the power of the Church fell under the rule of the

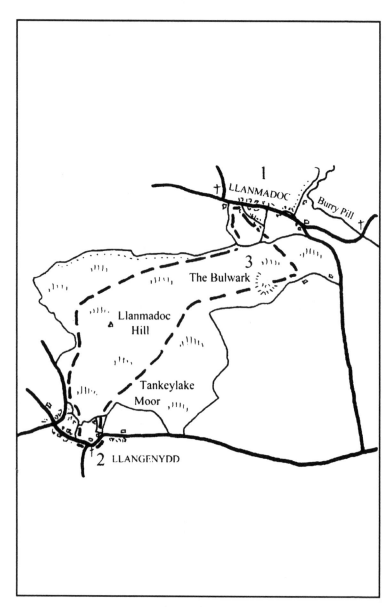

1 LLANMADOC

Burry Pill

3

The Bulwark

Llanmadoc
Hill

Tankeylake
Moor

2 LLANGENYDD

English King Henry VIII. Unlike the Knights Templars, the Knights Hospitallers have survived the centuries, and it is now a religious community within the Catholic church, continuing to manage hospitals and care for refugees as it once did in the Holy Land.

The present church, the smallest in Gower, dates from the 13th century. On restoration in the 1860s traces of medieval wall paintings and text were discovered on some of the fallen plaster by the Rev JD Davies, rector here and at nearby Cheriton from 1860-1911. Those he could distinguish he recorded. A staunch Anglo-Catholic in a none too Anglo-Catholic area, his dress and services were known to raise eyebrows! A talented wood carver - he carved the altar here, and left further examples of his talent at Cheriton church – he was also a tireless chronicler and observer of Gower life, finding time to produce a four volume *History of West Gower* from 1877-1894. As to be expected most of the area's economy has been linked with the vagaries of agriculture

Llanmadoc Church

and patterns of land ownership, though the 19th century witnessed strong links with the sea. Limestone from local quarries was shipped to Cornwall and Devon, with imports of coal and culm from nearby Loughor (Llwchwr) and Llanelli. At it's peak during the 1830s/1840s there were some thirty ships involved in the trade. The harbour was a rough and ready job, and the difficulties of navigating the winding and narrow pill to reach it were offset by guidance markers set in the banks.

2.   Llangenydd is very much a village patterned along Norman lines, with church and domestic dwellings grouped around the green. Though there has been much recent building this remains the centre of the village. The church, the largest in Gower, dates from the early 12th century and is dedicated to Gower's own saint, Cenydd, who reputedly founded a hermitage here in the 6th century. Sacked by the Vikings in 986 it was refounded, with revenue passing to Normandy. In 1414 Henry V seized all revenues of 'foreign' priories, including Llangenydd's, to help fund his wars with France – Agincourt was to be fought the following year. Henry later granted, for services rendered, a pension out of the proceeds of Llangenydd to a knight with one of the finest names in Gower history – Sir Hortonk van Klux. In 1442 Sir Hortonk's revenue passed to All Souls College, Oxford, then being built by Henry VI as a memorial to those killed in the Hundred Years War, the grant remaining until 1838. The church's lych gate, the only such in Gower, dates from 1903, and depicts carvings of scenes from St Cenydd's life. Inside the church is a 14th century effigy of a knight, one of the de la Mere family, but referred to locally as the 'Dolly Mare'. There are also three carved stone coffin lids set in the west wall, one pre-Norman and reputedly once the marker of St Cenydd's grave.

St Cenydd's Tale

6th century St Cenydd, Gower's own saint, was born the son of Dihocus, a prince of Brittany, whilst his parents were on a visit to Arthur's court at nearby Loughor (Llwchwr). Whatever the right or wrong of it his mother was his father's daughter, and it was said that when the baby was found to have been born with his calf twisted back on his thigh that it was a divine punishment. Fearing exposure the Prince placed the unwanted baby, Moses like, to float in a cot on the waters of the Burry Inlet. However Gower seagulls are not as

70

cruel as man, and noticing the baby's plight as he braved the stormy sea carried him, cradle and all, to nearby Pen Pyrod (Worm's Head) where he was given a surer home amongst a hollow of rock, and where they could use their wings to protect him from the vagaries of the weather.

After nine days an angel appeared and placed a breast-shaped bell in his mouth, through which he was miraculously fed on sweet milk. Cenydd's titty bell, as it came to be called, was kept replenished through the years by a doe. Taught by an angel until he was eighteen he was then directed to Llangenydd where he built his hut on the site now occupied by the village green. A spring, one of many that sprang forth where he rested, immediately gushed out to keep him refreshed. His titty bell he kept with him; it was common practice for saints to have a sacred bell, and he used his to enact many miracles.

Until quite recently most Gower villages had saint's day feasts, known as *Mabsant*. Llangenydd's was on 5 July, with dancing and fist-fighting, and with booths lining the green. Ale and whitepot were served; whitepot was a mixture of milk, flour and currants baked in a bread oven, and was said to be a reminder of the milk supplied to St Cenydd by his doe. A wooden cock dressed up in feathers of ribbons was hoisted to the top of the church tower as a representation of the seagulls – the holes made to hold the pole are still there should any wish to revive the custom!

3. It is easy to see why this site was chosen by Bronze and Iron Age peoples. With fabulous views over the peninsula with it's sandstone ridges and hills, and with views to Devon and Cornwall on one hand, and the sweep of Carmarthen Bay and the Burry Inlet on the other, it's geographical prominence and strategic importance would have been clear. Bronze Age peoples favoured siting funeral cairns in prominent positions so that they would be noticed, in a way integrating their presence into the living landscape in which the Bronze Age people lived. The Iron Age fort, the second largest in Gower after nearby Cil Ifor, shows evidence of several stages of construction, with three lines of defensive bulwarks, each with it's own entrance. Perhaps initially designed to protect cattle, it's human possibilities would have been soon recognised. There was at least one bloody battle in which Tonkin,

71

leader at the Bulwark, was killed in battle with the denizens of nearby Hardings Down. Blood swam above their boots it is said, and the site of the battle became known as Tankeylake moor. The hill has served more modern uses too. At the height of the Napoleonic wars when Royal Navy press-gangs set out from Llanelli for fresh deck hands, a watch was kept for the coming of the boat, and on the alarm being raised the able bodied young from the villages and farms below would hide in the caves at the Iron Age fort of North Hill Tor, overlooking Burry pill. The Bulwark was also the setting for the last scene in the strange case of the Santa Clause burglar. In the early 18th century one George Thomas had attempted to burgle Llanmadoc rectory, long since demolished, and was found dead in the chimney. He was buried in unconsecrated ground within the ramparts here.

The Burry Inlet and Loughor (Llwchwr) estuary is an extensive area of sand, mud flats and grazed saltmarsh. A shallow drowned river valley, it is of international importance for birds and has been designated a Ramsar site and a Special Protection Area (SPA). It has internationally important populations of pintail and oystercatchers, with large numbers of dark bellied brent geese, teal, widgeon, lapwing, curlew and redshank. There are major roosts for wildfowl at Penclawdd and Whiteford; and for waders along the north shore and on Llanrhidian marsh. The most important feeding areas are on the

southern shore on Llanrhidian sands and Penclawdd. The estuary itself is some 15miles/24 kilometres in length. The northern shore is, or has been, predominantly industrial, with harbour walls and factory complexes, and some saltmarsh at Pen-bre (Pembrey) and east of Llanelli. Opened in 2000 is the Millennium Coastal Park Llanelli, a 14 mile/22 kilometres environmental project that includes a floating harbour, watersports and indoor arenas, as well as the development of 80 hectares of what is one of the most important new wetlands in Europe. There is a cycleway and footpath linking all sites. The southern shore by contrast is mud and sand, backed by saltmarsh. The rich feeding grounds at Penclawdd have supported one of the largest cockle fisheries in Britain from pre-Roman times, and has always been the province of the local women. Before a channel was dredged to Llanelli, it was possible to cross the estuary from near Whiteford lighthouse by causeway to Burry Port. John Wesley, the Methodist, recalled crossing on horseback in 1764; even with a guide it took some four hours. The lighthouse, one of the few cast iron lighthouses left in the world, was erected in 1854 in response to the developing tinplate and coal industries on the north shore. It has been disused since 1933.

Walk Directions   [-] denotes Point of Interest

1. From the centre of Llanmadoc **[1]** walk past the shop towards the church. Turn left at the green and take the track leading straight ahead and uphill, signposted Llangenydd.

2. After a short distance bear right onto a distinct path leading around Llanmadoc hill – if you find yourself heading downhill on the path adjacent to the wall you are heading in the wrong direction towards Broughton Bay! Good views of Burry Inlet and Whiteford Tower.

3. After approximately 1 mile/1.5 kilometres there are paths leading up left to the trig point. Continue on the path until after $1/2$ mile/0.75 kilometres the path meets a wide path. Cross the path and go ahead left on a path leading through bracken and keep bearing down right to reach Llangenydd **[2]**.

4. Leave the village, passing the Kings Head, and where the road bends sharp right cross a stile left into a field. Cross the field and rejoin the path on Llanmadoc hill. Bear right and follow paths which lead to the Bulwark **[3]**.

5. Follow the path through the Bulwark, and where it meets a track bear left and follow it until, where it bends right, you leave it to follow a path leading down to Llanmadoc and the starting point.

Facilities

Shop, Post Office and pub in Llanmadoc and Llangenydd. Gallery in Llangenydd. Whiteford nature reserve – there is an excellent 4 mile circular walk from Llanmadoc taking in Whiteford Bay Leisure Park/Hills, Broughton Bay dunes and beach, then along the foot of

Cwm Ivy tor and through the pines along the marsh edge, returning to Llanmadoc along the 17th century sea wall. If you have never been a fan of pine trees this one may change your mind! It is possible to walk out to the lighthouse, though care should be taken with the tides.

Rhossili – Rhossili Downs – Hillend - Llangenydd – Hardings Down – Kingshall – Fernhill Farm – Middleton – Mewslade Bay – Tears Point – Rhossili

OS Maps:	1:50 000 Swansea & Gower 159; 1:25 000 Explorer 10 Gower.
Start:	Rhossili.
Access:	Rhossili lies at the end of the B4247, which in turn leads off from the A4118 Swansea to Port Eynon road. Buses 18A/18D from Swansea (Abertawe) to Rhossili.
Parking:	Car park at Rhossili – fee paying in season. Also small car park by the church.
Grade:	Strenuous – short sharp ascent to Rhossili Downs, and again a sharp descent to Hillend.

Points of Interest:

1. Rhossili over the years has had any number of variations in it's spelling; Rose-Hilly, Rhosheli, Rhoslley and Rhossilly have all been used. The most popular contender and explanation is Rhossili, that is *rhos*, or moor of *Sili*, Sili being Sulien, a Celtic saint to whom Rhossili's original church may have been dedicated. The present village, the most westerly in Gower, is not the first to bear the name. At the foot of Rhossili Downs, facing the sea, and tucked in between the isolated splendour of the remote and solitary Rectory, and the sheltered southern edge of Rhossili Bay is the Warren. It has always been known that there had been a church in the Warren, and ruins and human skeletons had been found. The heavy rains of the winter of 1979-80 caused erosion of the sand dunes revealing stone walls and more bones. On excavation, several houses – one showing indications of burnt thatching from the roof – and the walls of the ancient church were uncovered. The cross wall between the church nave and chancel showed paintings of red cinquefoil with black tendrils set within red and black lines with, running around the inside of the nave, stone

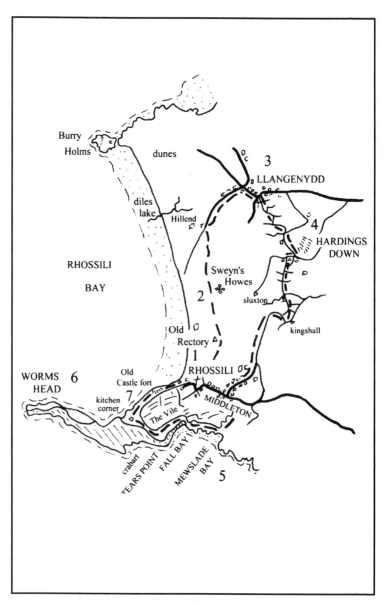

benches. It was long rumoured that the doorway of the present church was taken from the old church, and excavation indicated that the chancel arch had been removed. To protect the area the site has been re-covered with sand. It seems that the village, like nearby Pennard Castle, suffered in the violent storms that smashed into the south Wales coast in the early 14th century, and had drowned and choked in sand. It is probable that the lost village pre-dated the arrival of the Normans in 1110, founded on the site of a monastic settlement dedicated to St Cynwal.

The present church is dedicated to St Mary and probably dates from the 14th century. The tower has an elegant saddle-back roof, but it's finest feature is the probably late 12th century Romanesque arch, now doorway, from the old church. It is the only one of it's kind in Gower and is rare in Wales. At the top of the left hand pillar is a scratch dial – a stick placed in the hole would have cast a shadow and told the time. This suggests that the porch is a later addition, for the doorway must have once been open to the sky. The church was restored twice in the 19th century. At the west end of the churchyard by a small entrance gate is a grassy area bare of memorial stones, and formerly where shipwrecked sailors were buried – there is a plaque marked 'Sailors Corner'. Inside is a fine memorial to Edgar Evans, born in nearby Middleton, who perished on Scott's ill-fated 1912 Antarctic adventure. Rhossili may have had two churches, but the chapel has had a strong presence here since the Cromwellian times of the mid 17th century, with a Methodist society probably founded during the late 18th century, and small chapels built by local hands in the immediate neighbourhood. The ill feeling between church and chapel which formed such a divide in village life has now much abated!

2.   Rhossili Downs seen from the approach path to Worms Head (Pen Pyrod) is one of the finest sights in Gower. Unlike the limestone plateau of most of Gower the downs, like all Gower's high land, is comprised of more resistant Old Red Sandstone. Acid, and boggy on it's lower slopes, it is host to a wide range of heathland communities, particularly the summit with it's moss and lichen species – the downs is a Site of Special Scientific Interest (SSSI) for it's botanical importance, and is in the hands of the National Trust. The Beacon, where the trig point is sited, is the highest point in Gower at 633 feet/193 metres. *En route* to Llangenydd are the remains of an old radar station on the slope facing the sea. Inland are Sweyn's Howes, two neolithic burial chambers

dating from 2500 BC. *How* is Old English for mound, *Sweyn* a Viking lord who reputedly also gave name to Swansea i.e. *Sweyn's Eye, ey* meaning island. Several cairns from the later Bronze Age can be picked out, scattered along the higher stretches.

The Old Rectory was a rectory for most of it's life, though now it is owned by the National Trust and let as holiday accommodation. Originally the site and surrounding land were part of the glebe of Rhossili – in the 13th century the old church in the Warren, together with several other Gower churches, was given to the Knights of the Hospital of St John of Jerusalem, and the Knights may have lived on the site where the Rectory now stands. It is known that there was a primitive building there in the early 18th century, which was subsequently rebuilt in the 1850s. It's return to favour owed much to it's position exactly halfway between the villages of Rhossili and Llangenydd. When the livings of the two parishes were combined it seemed the perfect choice.

3. Llangenydd, named after Gower's own saint St Cenydd, effectively acts, with nearby Llanmadoc, as the gateway to north Gower. Traditionally the boundary between north and south is seen as Diles Lake, the stream that flows out roughly halfway along Rhossili's sands – *lake* is an old Gower word for a stream. Llangenydd gives access to Hillend, Llangenydd and Broughton Burrows, a fine area of dunes which cut off Rhossili Bay from the sands of Broughton. The tidal island of Burry Holms beyond the dunes, framing the bay, is bisected by an Iron Age earthwork. There are the ruins of a medieval chapel on the island, and it is believed to have been a site of pilgrimage, with it's shrine dedicated to St Cenydd. At the far end is the circular base of the now demolished automatic light that replaced Whiteford lighthouse.

4. Hardings Down, like Rhossili Downs and Llanmadoc hill, is formed from the Old Red Sandstone that has proved less susceptible to erosion than the underlying limestone. It's summit lies at just over 500 feet (157 metres) and is covered by 2 prominent earthbanks.

5. Mewslade Bay, like it's neighbour Fall Bay, is one of the most popular and safe bathing beaches of Gower. In Gower dialect a *slade* (Old English *slaed* or low valley) is a dry grassy valley running down to the sea; *mew* is the local word for seagull – there are colonies of kittiwakes who find the limestone crevices particularly favourable. At nearly 200 feet/656 metres Thurba Head towers over Mewslade; yet

Brandy for the Parson . . .

Rhossili Bay's wide 3 mile sweep of sand looks innocent enough nowadays, but in the 18th and early 19th centuries it was a haven for smugglers. With communications largely dependent on the sea – it was a rich man who could afford a horse to travel Gower's broken and pitted roads – the attraction of cheap cargoes landed away from the eyes of officialdom was attractive to most Gower people. Typically the smugglers' ships were fast sloops, capable of discharging cargo fast and cleanly onto the sands, and often outward bound from the ports of the Channel Islands and France. Once ashore the cargo, liquor or tea or luxury goods, were 'spirited' away to a safe haven – to the back of the Rectory was a cellar built into the hillside and running under the bed of the stream. Smuggling was rife all along the coast from the Burry Inlet to Brandy Cove by Caswell Bay and beyond, with anything up to a hundred men being involved in major operations – enough to deter the keenest excisemen. One oft quoted Customs report from 1795 notes at least 5000 kegs of brandy coming ashore between Burry Inlet and Mumbles over a six month period. With the formation of the Coastguard service in the early 19th century, with the end of the Napoleonic wars and a blockade of the Bristol Channel by navy patrols, Gower's smuggling days were effectively over.

Hand in glove with the smugglers' activities went those of the wreckers, though how prevalent wrecking was is uncertain. Certainly pirates were rife on the seaways of the Bristol Channel during medieval and Tudor times, and well laden ships would have been attractive targets to those on shore as well as those at sea. It would have been all too easy to hang a light on a cow's horn, or for a man or child to walk back and forwards with a lantern along the cliff's edge to lure ships in to a 'safe' haven. One apocryphal Victorian melodrama tells in ballad form the story of a 14 year old orphan girl who, in the early 18th century, had to earn her keep by carrying a light back and forth on Worms Head. Unable to reconcile her actions with her Christian beliefs she chose Easter 1712 to warn her last intended victim by lighting a brushwood fire as a beacon to indicate the secret danger of the rocks, only to be killed for her charity by the wreckers.

In the days of sail too many ships found themselves torn off course by the heavy winter winds and gales of Carmarthen Bay. The skeleton of the barque *Helvetia*, once laden with timber, still poke up from the sand at the Rhossili end of the bay from where she went down in 1887; by the island of Burry Holms low tide reveals the remains of the paddle steamer *City of Bristol* blown onto the sands in 1840, *en route* from Waterford in Ireland to Bristol, with the loss of all but two on board. To the left of the path as it ascends Rhossili Downs from the village is an isolated building, the Rocket house, which once housed the rocket apparatus used by local volunteers. The rocket itself, with line attached, was fired from shore to the stuttering ship, fastened to the mast, and the crew hauled out from the cauldron to safety in a breeches buoy. The worst shipwreck of all occurred in 1868 in Broughton Bay. Some eighteen or nineteen vessels laden with coal had been towed out by tugs from Llanelli and were waiting at anchor by Whiteford Point for the tide to turn, only to be smashed to pieces by an incoming swell – only two survived.

Wrecks provided a much welcomed bonus in timber and coal, with the occasional exotic cargo of fruit, wine, even ivory and silver dollars. The so called Dollar Ship is Rhossili's most famous wreck. Wrecked in the bay in the late 17th century she carried a cargo of silver dollars and pieces of eight, most dating from 1625 to 1639, a number of which came to light in 1807 at an exceptionally low tide. It has been suggested that the ship carried the dowry of either Catherine of Braganza, future Queen of Charles II, or else that of a Spanish princess betrothed to an English gentleman. There were further finds in 1833. Finds of Portuguese coins at nearby Bluepool Bay by Broughton Bay have suggested the wreckage of a second treasure ship, perhaps wrecked at the same time as the Dollar Ship.

most impressive are Jackies Tor, Devil's Truck and Lewes Castle which impose their magnificent presence over the sands. The wave cut platforms of Tears Point mark the edge of Fall Bay. At low tide it is possible to walk from Mewslade over to Fall Bay, but at high tide both beaches disappear!

6. Once past Tears Point lies the magnificent promontory of Worms Head. Probably Gower's most famous image the Inner, Middle and

Rhossili Downs and the Rectory

Outer Heads really do snake out into Carmarthen Bay like a serpent ready to slip away to sea. Accessible only at low tide there is a different atmosphere here. During the centuries sheep have been grazed and have always been regarded as providing the tastiest mutton in Gower – one local family if resident in London had a live sheep especially delivered in it's own travelling box. The mile long strip of land is now a national nature reserve managed by the National Trust. It is one of the principal seabird colonies of Carmarthen Bay, a breeding site for chough, guillemot, razorbill and kittiwake – there is restricted access to the Outer Head for this reason from mid March to mid July. Outside these months the Outer Head provides an ideal platform for watching seals and seabirds. Such a lonely and remote spot has bred many tales. John Leland, writing in 1540, noted a *'Hole at the Poynte of the Worme Heade . . . and Men fable there that a dore within the spatius Hole hathe be sene with great nayles on it'*. A blowhole there is, and a bone cave where remains of reindeer, cave bear, rhinoceros and mammoth have been found, but Leland believed in a tunnel that ran from the Worm under Carmarthen Bay to the Gwendraeth estuary by Kidwelly. Dylan Thomas used to visit, writing of the *'monstrous, thick grass there that made us spring-heeled, and we laughed and bounced on it, scaring the sheep . . . '* Access across the Shipway, or to the crabbing grounds of Crabart, is restricted to $2^1/2$ hours each side of low tide – tide times are displayed at the old coastguard hut, and at the National Trust shop in Rhossili.

7. To the right of the path leading back to Rhossili, and occupying the fertile and frost free peninsula between Rhossili and Tears Point, is the Vile (also spelt Viel), a fossilised medieval field system owing it's origins to the Norman system of land tenure – *vile* is the old Gower name for a field. Each person was allocated strips in different parts of the Vile, mixing good and 'bad' land fairly. Each strip was separated by a low bank and was distinguished by name eg Bramble Bush, Priest Hay and Sandyland. Nowadays many of the fields have been amalgamated, but the original patterns are still traceable. The area produces good early potatoes, together with corn, swedes and cauliflower. Old Castle fort, overlooking Rhossili Bay halfway between the coastguard hut and the hotel, is Iron Age in origin, roughly dating from 100BC to 100AD, and is protected by ditch and bank. However the fort has been much disturbed by the limestone quarrying which cut apart the cliffs from Old Castle fort down to Kitchen Corner for well

over two centuries. Each quarryman had his own quar or flotquar (floating quarry), working and loading from ledges cut into the rock. The cut limestone was loaded from the ledges into waiting Devon ships for export to Devon and Cornwall. Loading was possible only at high tide, and only in summer, and much skill was demanded of the Masters of the vessels to avoid smashing into the rocks. However the coming of the railways spelt the end of the seaborne trade, the last ships loading and leaving in 1899. One enterprising fisherman built himself a boathouse on one of the ledges at Kitchen Corner early in the 1900s, and it still survives in good condition.

Walk Directions   [-] denotes Point of Interest

1. Starting in Rhossili [1] walk past the church and take the track leading off from the main road and continue downhill to the access gate to Rhossili Downs.

2. Continue past the old Rocket house on the left up steps and path to reach the trig point, and continue across the downs [2], passing the neolithic Sweyn's Howes burial chambers *en route*, to finally reach Hillend Caravan and Camping Park.

3. Turn right and follow the road into Llangenydd [3].

4. Take the path to the left of the church grounds, cross a stone stile and cross three fields keeping to the right field edge.

5. Keep left in the fourth and fifth fields to enter a 'scrubby' sixth – ascend diagonally right a short steep path to join a farm track. Turn right, go through a gate and join the farm track leading around Hardings Down [4].

6. Continue on the track past the farm below right, until another track leading back sharp right and downhill is met.

7. Turn right onto the track and, where the track bears left, continue ahead until just past a large 'farm trail' sign; turn left off the track to reach a stile giving access to an old derelict building.

8. Continue through the ruins, and keeping to the right edge cross three fields, follow the left edge of a fourth, and then follow the right edge of two more to enter another field by a pond. Cross to reach the track by Kingshall.

9. Turn right onto the track and follow it as it leads you left back to

Rhossili Downs. Continue on this track past Fernhill farm to eventually join the main road at Middleton.

10. Turn left at the main road, cross, and shortly turn right onto a path/green lane. There is a yellow waymark on the back of the road sign, and a community council notice board and Caravan Club sign on the building on the corner by the path.

11. Continue on the path and go through a gate giving access to Mewslade Bay [5]. Stay on the top path by the wall overlooking the valley, and continue on the coastal path to Fall Bay and Tears Point. (If the tide is well out it is possible to walk along the beach to Tears Point). Mewslade is well worth the extra effort of a side visit!

12. Follow the path as it turns right, and then right again to lead you on the well trodden path from the cliff overlooking the Worms Head [6] back to Rhossili, passing the Vile and Old Castle fort *en route* [7].

Facilities

Most available in Rhossili and Llangennydd. National Trust visitors centre in Rhossili. BT telephones at Middleton, Rhossili and Llangenydd.

Port Eynon – Overton Mere – Long Hole Cliff – Foxhole Slade – The Knave – Thurba – Great Pitton Farm – West Pilton – East Pilton – Paviland Manor – Hills – Overton – Port Eynon

OS Maps: 1:50 000 Swansea & Gower 159; 1:25 000 Explorer 10 Gower.

Start: Port Eynon.

Access: Port Eynon is at the end of the A4118 main road through Gower. Bus 18A Swansea (Abertawe) to Port Eynon operates Monday to Saturday.

Parking: Car park in Port Eynon. Parking also possible at Great Pitton farm.

Grade: Strenuous.

Points of Interest:

1. Port Eynon derives it's name from Eynon, or Einion, an 11th century prince. A popular village life now tends to centre around the whitewashed cottages and sandy foreshore; however in 19th century Port Eynon and earlier the centre of gravity was closer out towards Port Eynon Point. The nearby oyster beds, thinned out probably by overfishing by 1870, provided a profitable winter trade with, at it's height from the 1830s to 1850s, some forty skiffs sailing out from the bay. Catches were landed at Crowder's Quay – the area between the youth hostel and the Salt House – for storage in pools before they were shipped out by fishing smacks to Bristol and Swansea, and on to other ports. The best beds were out south of the Helwick Sands buoy. A 1674 survey noted that Port Eynon's oysters were the best in Britain. The season lasted from September to early March; the summer months were devoted to quarrying the limestone cliffs which look down towards the village and the sea. Once cut the limestone blocks were taken to the shore by cart and laid out in two parallel lines – the apex marked by a wooden pole which is still visible. Guided by the pole, ships, usually from the Devon ports of Bideford and Barnstable, would

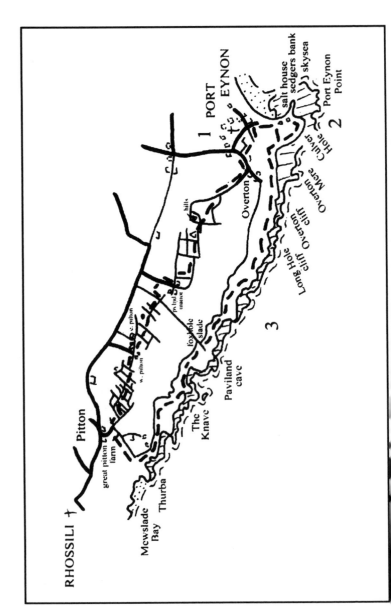

row in between the lines at high tide, anchor, and wait for low tide for beaching and loading. The blue-green stones brought over as ballast still litter the beach.

Inevitably the tides and winds around the Gower coast have proved treacherous to shipping. There were lifeboat teams in the larger villages who would fire out rocket lines from the shore to distressed ships and haul in survivors, but the wreck of the *Agnes Jack* in 1883 raised sufficient concern for the establishment of a permanent lifeboat station in 1884; *A Daughter's Offering* the first lifeboat. The *Agnes Jack* had been on her way from Swansea to Llanelli with a cargo of lead ore when she foundered off Port Eynon Point. First light showed twenty crew and one passenger clinging to the mast – all that remained of the ship above the water; the rocket lines fired out to them failed to reach, and all drowned. 1906 saw the introduction of a new 35 foot lifeboat, the *Janet*, built with a draught of just over 2 feet to enable her to be launched in the shallow water. It must have been a fine sight to see her launched in a heavy sea; she was towed down the lifeboat ramp by local farm horses; men, crew and horses fighting for balance in the flying surf. The end for the lifeboat came in 1916 when she was launched to aid the Glasgow steamer *Dunvegan*, aground at Oxwich Point. Heavy breakers meant that *Janet* could not reach the ship, and she turned for home, only for the wind to turn her towards Pwlldu Head. Capsizing twice, three of her crew drowned. After this the lifeboat station was closed, and the *Janet* transferred to Stornoway in the Scottish Hebrides. A white marble statue was erected in Port Eynon's church in memory of the lost men. The lifeboat station is now the local youth hostel.

Beyond the youth hostel and Crowder's Quay are the ruined walls of two 18th to 19th century cottages which were homes for some 100/150 years to oyster fishing families, the reservoir below belongs to the late 16th century Salt House. The water here is highly saline, and it is known that a salt works, one of the most advanced for it's time, was in existence by 1598, continuing in use for some fifty years. Seawater was allowed to enter the reservoir for refining in the pan house which stood above. Traditionally the Salt House has always been connected to the Lucas family, one of the many families to have come to prominence in Gower's long history. The first in the family line was Geoffrey, arriving from Essex circa 1450. It was David Lucas who, during the reign of Henry VIII, was said to have built the original mansion here –

possibly on the site of an earlier Norman castle – for his son John. John Lucas was a wild and violent man who had spent his youth soldiering and exploring the world. Returning to marriage and a new mansion he teamed up with other prominent local youths from, among others, the Mansels and Scurlages, and took to a life of piracy and wrecking, succouring *'ye privates and ye French smugglers'* as the expression of the day has it. He fortified the mansion with battlements and extended the house back to the cliffs. The mansion was stocked with arms, the cellars with liquor. He passed many of the fruits of his labour on to local Gower people, his profitable business to his son Phillip on his death. It is said, perhaps with a salty tongue in the cheek, that Gilbert and Sullivan's comic opera *The Pirates of Penzance* is based on his life.

The Salt House remained in the Lucas family for seven generations, until the death of another John Lucas at the beginning of the 18th century. It was this last John Lucas who brought an air of legality to the house. He discovered that when the local iron stained millstone grit was ground down materials were produced which could be used in the manufacture of paint, materials which he soon exported by his own small fleet of skiffs to Cardiff and Bristol. In 1703 one of the worst storms in Gower's history struck the coast; the Salt House itself was cracked open by the sea and the cellars flooded, and Lucas' skiffs flung on to the shore, and as final punishment the house was spat at by lightning. At the time it is said that John Lucas lay dying, shortly to be buried at Sedger Bank in defiance of the sea. The later cottages were abandoned in the 1880s when the encroaching sand rose too high.

2. No trip to Port Eynon Point would be complete without a visit to Culver Hole. Unique in Britain, Culver Hole has long been a place of mystery. In a cleft of rock *en route* to Overton Mere a sixty foot wall of limestone blocks has been built, effectively creating a chamber cut off from the sea. Ten foot thick at the base, with two rectangular windows at the bottom and two circular at the top it even has a flight of steps, though there is no evidence of there ever having been any floors. Probably the key to it's origins lie in the name *culver*; the old English word for pigeon. Inside are a series of rectangular holes common to dovecotes, and though no trace of it exists, there may have been a castle nearby during early Norman times – pigeons were introduced as a supplement to the Norman diet. Records note it's existence as early as the 13th century, and it is known that John Lucas (the first) repaired it and used it as a stronghold and storage area, probably for explosives –

88

The Knave

rumours have persisted that an underground passage leads from Culver Hole to the old Salt House. Just along from Culver Hole is a bone cave where remains of woolly rhinoceros, mammoth and red deer have been found. Off the point are Sedgers Bank and Skysea, both islands at high tide – Sedgers Bank and Port Eynon Point are both nature reserves managed by the Glamorgan Wildlife Trust. The rocky foreshore has long been popular lobster and crabbing grounds. Port Eynon Point is a regionally important site for shearwater and gannet watching in July and August. Out at sea, marked by a line of broken water at low tides, are the Helwick Sands, marked to prevent mishap – the first light vessel was in place by 1846. Finds of horseshoes on the sands have suggested that there was once a roadway here, before the sea rose to cover it.

3. The section of cliffs from Overton Mere to the Worm's Head is often referred to as *the Magnificent Five Miles*. One of the finest coastal areas in Britain the cliff paths climb up the spines of the limestone ridges, to

drop down into narrow valleys or *slades*. All have names descriptive of their natural charm – Red Gut, Groaning Slade, Black Hole Gut, Ram Grove, Butter Slade, Yellow Top. There are disused quarries, ruins of old limekilns and Iron Age promontory forts. Cormorants perch on the small rocky islands, wings stretched out to welcome the sun. The Knave, towards Thurba Head, is a superb rock formation climbing out of the sea, a spectacular sight with the waves crashing around him, whilst Thurba Head is the most precipitous of the cliffs in Gower. The whole stretch is pitted with caves where hyenas dragged in remains of mammoth and woolly rhinoceros, competing with early man for shelter as the ice sheets retreated and advanced. There are some famous bone caves along this limestone coast; all have been excavated. Paviland, by Foxhole Slade, is world famous, though access is difficult, Deborah's Hole by the Knave, and Long Hole cave, are easily entered. Long Hole cave, high up in a small limestone cliff, was first excavated in the 1860s, further excavations confirmed use by man in upper Palaeolithic times. The cave has had many names carved into the rock by visitors, some dating back to the 1880s. If you climb up and look out from within, it will provide a fine view over the foreshore and the

The Red Lady of Paviland

Paviland cave, more properly known as Goat's Hole, came to world attention with the discovery and excavation in 1823 of the first human fossil in Europe. Situated in a cleft in the cliff face below Yellow Top – the latter so called because of the yellow and orange lichen on the upper rocks – this small teardrop shaped cave peers out across the Bristol Channel and the mists of time. The local discovery of a cave full of bones reached the ears of the Reverend William Buckland, appointed first professor of geology at Oxford in 1819, and a future Dean of Westminster. Buckland was one of the great Victorians, fired with enthusiasms and full of eccentricities. Having made a spectacular find of animal bones in a cave at Kirkdale in Yorkshire in 1820 he noticed the predominance of those of hyenas. To test the characteristic teeth marks and crushing of the other bones by the hyenas he kept a pet hyena called Billy for comparison of behaviour. His dinner parties were often entertaining – he was known to serve up the odd panther chop or grilled alligator – and on one occasion his guests were much distressed by the information that the crunching emanating from beneath the sofa was only Billy eating one of the guinea pigs. He was known to leap into excavation sites in top hat and gown, with arms flailing. At Paviland he was forced to bend.

His excavation was meticulous. What he unearthed was a headless skeleton, with the bones stained with red ochre, and accompanied by bone, antler and ivory goods, including sea-shell necklaces, and an abundance of worked flints. There were also present bones from mammoth and woolly rhinoceros. A firm believer in the deluge theory – he published in 1823 a paper on . . . *Geological Phenomena, Attending the Action of an Universal Deluge*, which declared a belief that the earth had been devastated by a universal flood. He also believed in the impossibility of the appearance of man before the time assigned to it in Genesis, dated by many clerics to 4004 BC – Buckland could not conceive of the antiquity of man. Accordingly he dated the discovery to Romano-British times, arguing for a ceremonial burial for a Roman prostitute or witch. He gave her the name *The Red Lady of Paviland*.

A more comprehensive evaluation was undertaken in 1912 by Sollas, a later professor of geology at Oxford. He noted that the body was that of a young man, and that the bones had been ritually stained with red ochre. Red ochre occurs naturally in Gower as in many parts of the world – at Red Chamber by the Knave the red ochre was once commercially extracted – and by 26,000 years ago many burials in western and eastern Europe were accompanied by red ochre powder, suggestive of ritual. Current carbon dating places the date of the young man to 26,000 years before present, long before the last glacial maximum of 18000 years ago. Gower, at the edge of the ice sheets, would not have been permanently inhabited, but existed on the periphery of the long distance social networks in which early man operated. The young man is still referred to as *The Red Lady of Paviland* – gender bending can persist for a long time in archaeology; perhaps as recompense *Swanscombe Man* from Kent has long been known to be a woman! Less important, and smaller, is Paviland Western cave, to the west, and above Goat's Hole.

encroaching sea – in prehistory the Bristol Channel would have been dry land bisected by a river. If you are lucky you may see the local kestrels hunting below you! The coastal stretch is owned by the National Trust, with nature reserves managed by the Glamorgan Wildlife Trust at Overton Mere, Overton Cliff, Long Hole Cliff and Deborah's Hole – their emblem is a male and female eider in flight.

Walk Directions   [-] denotes Point of Interest

1. Starting from Port Eynon **[1]** choice of routes to Overton Mere – either continue from the car park passed the Salt House, visiting Culver Hole **[2]** *en route*, and then ascending the headland to pass the memorial stone; or turn right onto the green lane in front of the youth hostel, and again right at the National Trust sign Port Eynon Point, to reach the top of the cliff overlooking Overton Mere. Descend to join the coastal path.

2. Continue on the coastal path to reach Glamorgan Wildlife Trust signs at Overton Cliff and Long Hole cliff **[3]**. Long Hole cave is above right in the cliff overlooking the path just before the Trust sign is reached – easy ascent up to the cave from the path.

3. From the sign at Long Hole cliff continue on the coastal path as it ascends passed turfed limekilns and stay on the path until a stile in a wall is crossed. Continue up the next ridge and down to the next valley – continue passed the row of fence posts to the next valley. From here, unless you wish to undertake a tricky rock traverse (you will recognise it if you have walked too far!) take the easy path leading up from the coastal path to join the cliff path.

4. Turn left and continue to the obvious gash of Foxhole Slade. Paviland cave is at the bottom of the slade, to the right – access at low tide and difficult.

5. Continue on the cliff path from Foxhole Slade, passing the route down to the Knave *en route*, to reach Thurba. At Thurba follow the line of the stone wall as it turns inland to meet a green lane/farm lane. At a farm track bear left and continue passed farm buildings to reach the farm road. Turn right – left will take you to Pitton.

6. Continue on the path to shortly turn left over a stile marked by a wooden marker with a blue tip. Continue on field paths to West Pilton. The route is marked for most of it's length by the wooden markers.

7. At West Pilton cross the road and continue directly ahead to reach a stile. Cross the stile and continue ahead, keeping East Pilton farm buildings on your left. Continue across fields, passing two farm ponds on your left – popular with the local herons! – to meet the path from Pilton Green to Foxhole Slade.

8. Turn left and where the path continues ahead across a footbridge turn right, keeping the stream to your left. Continue to reach the road to Paviland Manor.

9. Turn right and continue to reach farm buildings. Turn left at the barn – walking man sign here – and once passed the barn bear right and continue along the field edge. Continue across fields, passing a trig point to the left, to reach the ruins of Hills. Stunning views inland over Gower and Carmarthenshire.

10. From Hills cross waymarked stiles and bear right downhill across a field to reach the path leading down to Overton.

11. At Overton turn left and continue until, just passed a farm on the right, steps lead up to a stile giving access to the route back down through a caravan site to Port Eynon below.

Facilities

Most available in Port Eynon. Youth hostel in Port Eynon.

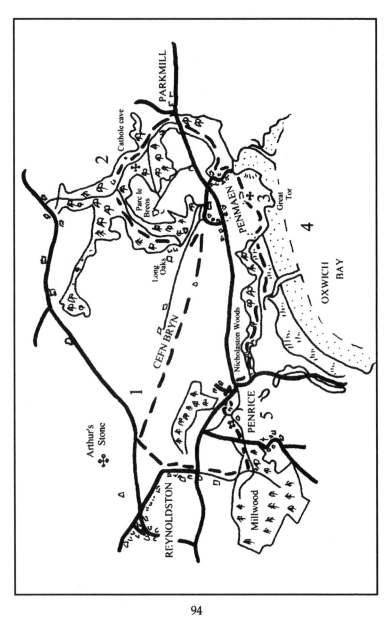

PARKMILL

Cathole cave

2

Parc le Breos

Long Oaks

CEFN BRYN

1

Arthur's Stone

REYNOLDSTON

Millwood

PENRICE

5

Nicholaston Woods

PENMAEN

3

Great Tor

4

OXWICH BAY

Cefn Bryn – Green Cwm – Notthill –
Three Cliffs Bay – Penmaen Burrows –
Nicholaston Burrows – Nicholaston Woods –
Penrice Castle – Millwood –
Little Reynoldston – Cefn Bryn

OS Maps:	1:50 000 Swansea & Gower 159; 1:25 000 Explorer 10 Gower.
Start:	Cefn Bryn.
Access:	The start point is situated on the summit of the minor road between the B4271 Llanrhidian to Upper Killay road and Reynoldston. Buses 18A from Swansea to Rhossili stop at Reynoldston; 18, 18A and 18D at Parkmill Shepherds.
Parking:	Parking possible on rough ground at the start point.
Grade:	Strenuous.

Points of Interest:

1. The long sandstone ridge of Cefn Bryn dominates Gower. 5 miles/8 kilometres in length it is bordered on it's western side by the Burry pill which meets the sea at the Burry Inlet. The northern slope is it's widest and wettest side, sloping down to face Carmarthenshire across the water, while the southern edge peers down over Oxwich and Three Cliffs Bay. It is highest at it's eastern side – at 609 feet/186 metres; it is Gower's second highest point after Rhossili Downs. It makes for a wild and bracing walk in winter with the frost crackling underfoot; in good weather it gives the lie of the land of Gower, it's greens and browns leading down to summer blues and yellows, and to the strict definition of the rocks at the edge of the sea. One member of the Mansel Talbot family from Penrice (Pen-rhys) used to lead his hounds home along the ridge after hunting in the Green Cwm and Parc le Breos, and the route has become known as Talbot's Way or Talbot's Road. Snaking across the ridge is the old sandstone Red Road, now tarmacked and leading up from Cilibion to Reynoldston. At one time coal carts from

Penclawdd in north Gower made their way up the *'coal road'* to supply southern Gower. By Cilibion is Broad Pool, one of Gower's largest inland areas of open water, and managed by the Glamorgan Naturalist Trust as a nature reserve. The occasional heron stands sentinel over the water lilies and the ducks, with the wild ponies for company.

Overlooking the Burry estuary, and one of Gower's most famous landmarks, is Arthur's Stone or Maen Ceti, one of the wonders of Old Britain. The Breton soldiers who accompanied Henry Tudor to Bosworth and the English crown diverted especially to see it. The capstone is possibly 25 tons and was originally bigger, and covers two burial chambers. It has been dated to 2500 BC in the neolithic era, though this date is now in doubt and the stone may be later. Some say that the stone has magical properties and that on Midsummer's eve it creeps down to the Burry estuary for a long cool drink. Others attribute it's origins to Arthur, who crossing Carmarthenshire on his way to Camlan threw a pebble out from his shoe to land and remain on Cefn Bryn. Reynoldston, Gower's highest village, lies at the crossroads of north and south Gower, and is a highly popular watering hole owing to the presence of King Arthur's hotel! A Norman village complete with village green, it takes it's name from 13th century Reginald or Reynold de Breos. The church, dedicated to St George, originally dates from the 13th century, and may have been founded on an earlier Celtic site. It was completely rebuilt in the 1860s.

2. Green Cwm was once part of the estate of Parc de Breos, sold in 1950. Much of the area is in the hands of the Forestry Commission, who have retained many of the original deciduous trees of ash and oak. The stream running through Green Cwm rises to the north on Welsh Moor, but at the boundary between the millstone grit and limestone the stream vanishes underground, in the process creating one of Gower's finest underground cave systems – the Great Hall itself being 200 feet high. The stream re-emerges by the junction of the path with the road to Parc le Breos. The Green Cwm holds two gems. Cathole cave is one of Gower's famous bone caves, the only major one inland, and easily accessible from the path. Excavation has produced evidence from Upper Palaeolithic, mesolithic and Bronze Age periods. The cave was certainly inhabited circa 12,000 BC, and there have been several finds of flint blades. The presence of the cave may have influenced the site for the Giants Grave; the neolithic burial chamber of Parc le Breos which lies almost opposite. First excavated in 1869 the remains of two

dozen people were found, together with animal bones and pottery fragments. Later excavations have recovered bones of a minimum of forty people, including children, and each burial chamber and the central passage would have housed a number of people. Radio carbon dating has put the time scale at 3800-3000 BC. In construction it is part of the Cotswold-Severn tradition. The chamber is wedge shaped, constructed from slabs of coarse limestone, and with a pronounced forecourt entrance. The structure would originally have been covered with further slabs, perhaps topped with a larger capstone. The site was laid out in it's present form following excavation in 1960/61.

3. Penmaen Burrows, with it's rich variety of habitats, has a few surprises hidden amongst the bracken hillocks and sand dunes. Pen-y-crug, in a small grassy clearing, is a passage grave dating from circa 3000 BC. Like Parc le Breos in Green Cwm it belongs to the Cotswold-Severn tradition. Part of the entrance passage, the central passage and south side chamber, with capstone, remain on view. First excavated in 1893 human and animal remains and pottery fragments were found. On the other side of the path from Pen-y-crug are the remains of a church which became, like Pennard Castle across Three Cliffs Bay, overwhelmed by sand. It was excavated in the 19th century when graves were uncovered. Much of southern Gower, like South Wales, was subjected to fierce sand storms during the 14th and 15th centuries, and it was then that the sands blown up from Oxwich formed the burrows and choked the church. It was long rumoured that beneath the burrows is the lost village of Steadworlango, however there is doubt now that it ever existed, except as a grand name for a mystery! All that now remains of the church is the stone wall depression.

Overlooking Three Cliffs Bay is a massive circular bank, all that remains of Castle Tower, an early 12th/13th century Norman ringwork castle. Excavated in 1961 it was found that the timber entrance tower had burnt down in a fire – the tower would originally have provided the main accommodation area, the entrance and fighting platform. The ringwork castle was a simpler form than the motte and bailey – a ditch and earthen rampart would have been protected by a timber palisade. There would no doubt have been smaller buildings within the ringwork to which the tower gave entrance. To enrich the Norman diet rabbits were kept for meat, and warrens, or pillow mounds, were constructed close by settlements – as was the case here. Great Tor, at 200 feet/61 metres, is the great limestone spur that divides, except at low tides, Three Cliffs Bay from Oxwich Bay. Leather's Hole, another of Gower's bone caves, lies close to the top and would have been a hyena den where the hyenas that once roamed the plain of the Bristol Channel in pre-history would have dragged the remains of mammoth, woolly rhinoceros and wolf. Access only for the brave!

4. Oxwich Bay's 2 mile stretch of golden sand make it one of Gower's most popular beaches. The bay is shallow, some 10 metres in depth over a rock and sand sea bed, and offers safe bathing. The area between Oxwich Point and Nicholaston pill, together with Crawley wood, comprise Oxwich national nature reserve; it is one of the finest coastal habitats in Britain, with reed swamp and saltmarshes, freshwater lakes, dunes, woodlands and cliffs. Much of the reserve is open access or woodland footpath, and is well worth exploring for the richness of it's rare plants, and for viewing the spring and early summer birds which make it their home. The reserve was established in 1963 in an agreement with Penrice estate. Oxwich village is one of the prettiest and most popular villages in Gower, still with thatched roof cottages along it's thin street.

5. Penrice Castle was originally one of the early Norman ringwork castles; known as Mounty Brook it was sited behind the present Penrice village – it's traces are still, just, visible from the wood below. Penrice (Pen-rhys) village was once one of the social centres of Gower, with twice weekly markets, and hiring fairs, and with organised fights and a well frequented inn. It is quieter now, and the inn has gone, but it still gives a flavour of old Gower – some fine carved stone faces look down over the church windows! The present stone castle was built in a more favourable position, away from the village, in the mid 13th century; the round keep constructed first circa 1240. The great gatehouse, the two large towers and curtain walls were added in the late 13th century. It became the largest and most impressive castle in Gower. A columbarium, or pigeon house, was added in 1500 – plump pigeon pie for the lords at table! By the 15th century the estate had passed from the de Penrice family to the Mansel family. Sir Rice Mansel abandoned Penrice Castle and, together with his son Edward, began work in the early 16th century on a new magnificent fortified manor house overlooking Oxwich Bay – Oxwich Castle.

In the 18th century the Mansel estates passed to the Talbot family, and the family name became Mansel Talbot. In the late 18th century Thomas Mansel Talbot built the present classical mansion in the shadows of the old Penrice Castle, furnishing it with Dutch and Italian paintings. To the new house he added a landscape garden in the English style, using the natural outlines and varying colours of the sea at Oxwich Bay as a fine backdrop. Trees and shrubs were introduced, vistas opened up, and the existing stream was dammed to make a number of small lakes. A sea wall excluded the sea from the inner marsh, with consequent improvements in grazing. The present road to Oxwich follows the wall of the 'Great Park' through the lakes; and the marshes, now mostly wild, are part of Oxwich national nature reserve. There is a well established heronry here. Christopher Rice Mansel Talbot – he of Talbot's Way on Cefn Bryn – carried on the work. The castle towers flanking the entrance to Penrice house are an 18th century folly built by Thomas Mansel Talbot!

Three Cliffs Bay and Pobbles Beach

Penrice House

Walk Directions   [-] denotes Point of Interest

1. From the start point **[1]** take the track leading off diagonally left – after a short distance there is a viewpoint pillar on the left on the track. The summit lies some 2 miles/3 kilometres away by the trig point and the grassed-over Cefn Bryn service reservoir.

2. Continue on the track from the summit to reach a T junction with a well defined track. Turn left and follow the track alongside woodland until, just before the track divides ahead by Long Oaks, cross a stile right into the wood.

3. Follow the main track down through Green Cwm to a four-way junction and take the right turn **[2]**. Just before the path bears towards the right there is Cathole cave in a limestone cliff on the left – a small path leads up to it.

4. Continue on, passing Parc

100

le Breos neolithic burial chamber on the right, to reach the road leading down to Parkmill.

5. Continue to the main road, cross and take the path – marked with a bridleway sign – opposite and right. Follow the well defined path uphill through woodland to reach North Hill farm – this was once the main road through Gower!

6. At the junction turn left downhill – National Trust sign here 'Notthill'. Follow the road until the tarmac ends by the last property on the right. There is a yellow BT 999 emergency phone at the corner.

7. Depending on the state of the tide in Three Cliffs Bay below either continue on the grit path ahead to reach stepping stones leading to Pobbles beach (do not cross the stones but keep to the right), or take the narrow path immediately right and continue downhill.

8. Either way, aim for the foot of Penmaen Burrows and take the obvious wide sandy path leading up through bracken to the headland. Once at the top take the path on the right – after a short distance there is a path leading off left to a neolithic burial chamber in a small clearing. Just over a small rise on the right of the main path is the shell of a ruined church [3].

9. Continue on the coastal route, passing two impressive and recently restored double-vented limekilns on the left, to reach an iron bar stile giving views over Oxwich and Nicholaston Burrows below [4].

10. Stay on the cliff path until a stile on the right, by farmland, is reached – do not cross the stile but take the path left down to reach an obvious sand track through the dunes to reach the base of the cliff point ahead.

11. Continue on the path to reach a Nature Reserve sign marking the entrance to Nicholaston Woods. Continue on the path through the woods, taking the left path when offered a choice.

12. Once at the road leading down to Oxwich, turn right uphill to the main road through Gower. Turn left and continue on the main road a short distance until the entrance to Penrice estate is reached. Cross by an old stone stile – walking man sign here – and follow the yellow markers down to a road. The first yellow marker is ahead and slightly right, away from the track.

13. Once at the road turn left and then right, following the road passed Penrice Castle [5] down to a minor road.

14. Cross the road and enter Millwood – there was a mill here on the left at one time, and the old pond has been reconstructed. Follow the permissive path highlighted by a green arrow and continue until a pond is reached. Once at the pond take the track on the right leading uphill to join a farm track leading back to the main Gower road.

15. Cross and continue on the road leading to Little Reynoldston. Where the road bends left to Reynoldston take a path on the right leading up through moorland to reach the starting point.

Facilities

Excellent inn at Reynoldston – the King Arthur hotel. Parkmill offers the Heritage Centre, and café, shop and petrol at Shepherds – Gower Inn close by. Oxwich has the Oxwich Bay hotel, overlooking the beach.

Parkmill – Ilston Cwm – Ilston – Lunnon – Parkmill

The walk can be linked with the Pennard walk (Walk 13) by using the footpath from Parkmill up to Pennard golf course.

OS Maps:	1:50 000 Swansea & Gower 159; 1:25 000 Explorer 10 Gower.
Start:	Gower Heritage Centre at Parkmill.
Access:	Parkmill is on the A4118 Swansea to Port Eynon road, and is 8 miles/12.75 kilometres from Swansea (Abertawe). Buses 18/18A/18D from Swansea stop at Parkmill Shepherds/Heritage Centre.
Parking:	Car park at the Heritage Centre – sited a short distance ahead on the minor road past Shepherds. Fee if not visiting the centre. If starting from Ilston, limited parking possible by the church or by the quarry.
Grade:	Easy.

Points of Interest:

1. Parkmill takes it's name from the working corn and saw mill that is now the heart of the Gower Heritage Centre. Built circa 1160 by the powerful Norman de Breos family it continues to grind corn for flour as it has always done, nowadays supplying the Centre's tearoom with cakes and bread. It is the last working mill left of what were once some fifty mills in Gower. Power to the mill comes from a leat run off from the stream running through Green Cwm. The stream itself unites just below the mill with the Ilston stream to form Pennard pill, running on to feed the sea at Three Cliffs Bay. Other rural crafts took advantage of the power of the wheel, and during the centuries following the mill's founding wheelwright, blacksmith and carpentry shops were added. The miller's cottage, to the right of the Centre's entrance, was built some 300 years ago by the 'resident' millers, the Davies family. Parkmill is one of the busy places of Gower; situated on the main route to Port Eynon and Rhossili, with the noted Gower Inn close by, and with quick access to the delights of Three Cliffs Bay, Green Cwm and Ilston Cwm.

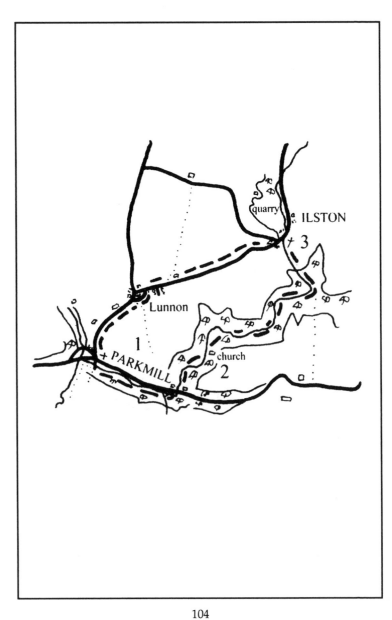

2. Ilston Cwm, like Green Cwm and Bishopston valley, is one of the rare survivals of the woodland that once covered all Gower. Their situation within steep sided valleys made them unattractive to agricultural development, and they have been allowed to retain their deciduous inheritance. Rising on Fairwood Common the stream running through Ilston Cwm is known locally as the *killy willy*, an expression also understood in the West Country of England, and meaning 'something that wanders from place to place'. The woods are cool and welcoming on hot days with, above, the sheltering trees and the blue murmur of the birds.

A short distance into the wood, and by a splendid wooden footbridge, are the ruins of the first Baptist church in Wales on what was once the site of the medieval Trinity Well chapel. There is a plaque commemorating the church's founding by John Myles, appointed minister at Ilston during the Commonwealth of 1649 to 1660. Myles, a Puritan intellectual with an Oxford education, had been expelled from the State church during the earlier reign of Charles I for refusing to read the Book of Sports from the pulpit as was required by law. Power and control in Stuart times was exercised locally as much by the minister in the pulpit as by 'secular' officialdom, and it was against the law not to attend church. Myles' refusal would have been seen as an affront to Stuart power. It is interesting to quote an extract from the Book of Sports – '*As for our good people's recreation, our pleasure is that after the end of Divine Service, our good people be not letted, disturbed or discouraged from any lawful recreation, such as Dancing, either man or woman, Archery for men, leaping, vaulting or any such harmless recreation, or from having Maypoles, Whitsun Ales or Morris dances, and the setting up of Maypoles and other Sports there with used'*. Myles' problems returned with the restoration of Charles II in 1660. The idea that a religion other than the State church could be chosen was seen as subversive; Quakers, Baptists, Independents and Presbyterians suffered persecution, Quakers particularly. Myles was replaced by the previous incumbent at Ilston, and in 1663 he, with his followers, emigrated to America, founding a Baptist church at Swansea, Massachusetts. The memorial in 1928 was well attended, with the choir dressed in Puritan style, and with a resounding speech by Lloyd George.

3. Ilston is a delightful village set alongside the Ilston stream, and hidden away from the main corners of Gower. The church, possibly on the site of an earlier Christian settlement, dates from the 13th century,

and is dedicated to the 6th century saint Illtud. John de Breos, in 1221, presented the church to the Knights Hospitallers of St John of Jerusalem who retained possession of it until the dissolution of the monasteries in 1540, when it passed to the Crown. There was a school attached to the church in the 18th century, but this soon fell into abeyance. Inside the church is a superb bell cast in 1520 and with an inscription to Thomas à Becket. Two other bells, cast by a local Oystermouth firm, date from circa 1776, and now hang in the tower. Just beyond the village the old quarry is now a nature reserve. The alternating limestone and clay beds are rare in Wales, and contain fossilised sea lilies. In 1933, when the quarry was still operative, a rare haul of buried treasure in the shape of a hoard of Roman coins was found – perhaps some long ago centurion had thought the site a safe hiding place!

Walk Directions   [-] denotes Point of Interest

1. Starting from the car park at the Gower Heritage Centre walk back up the road to Shepherds shop and café [1].

2. Cross the main road, and take the path leading across a footbridge, turn left, and follow the level path through the wood to reach a minor road. Cross the minor road, and take the path across the footbridge to the main road.

3. Turn right, continue past the West Glamorgan Guides Activity Centre and, just before the Gower Inn, take a signposted path on the left indicating Ilston 2 kilometres.

4. After the second, wooden, footbridge there are the ruins on the right of the first Baptist church in Wales, with a plaque commemorating it's passing [2].

5. Continue through the wood, crossing several footbridges, until a crossroads of paths is met – those leading ahead and joining from the right are less well defined.

6. Bear left and, with the stream on the left, continue until entry into Ilston church grounds is joined through a kissing gate.

7. Continue through the church grounds to join the road through the village [3] – option here to turn right to visit the nature reserve at the disused quarry, or to turn left and continue uphill on the road to reach Lunnon.

Ilston Church

8. At Lunnon turn left and follow the road down to Parkmill (Shepherds) and the starting point.

Facilities

Gower Heritage Centre at Parkmill – tearoom, craft worskshops, puppet theatre; also a range of events held throughout the year. Shop, newsagents and café, also petrol, at Shepherds. Gower Inn – a popular local watering hole and eating place – nearby.

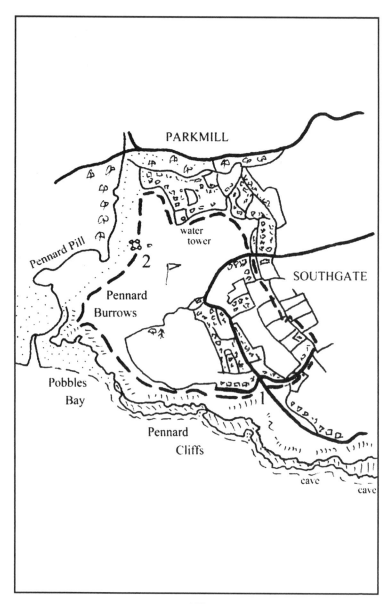

PARKMILL

Pennard Pill

water
tower

2

Pennard
Burrows

SOUTHGATE

Pobbles
Bay

Pennard
Cliffs

1

cave

cave

Southgate – Pennard Burrows –
Pennard Castle – Southgate

Can be combined with the Ilston walk (Walk 12) by using the link path between the golf course and Parkmill.

OS Maps:	1:50 000 Swansea & Gower 159; Explorer 10 Gower.
Start:	Southgate.
Access:	Southgate can be reached from the B4436 Kittle to Swansea (Abertawe) road. Bus 18D on weekdays, 14 on Sundays: Swansea (Abertawe) – Pennard Cliffs.
Parking:	National Trust car park at Southgate – small fee if not a Trust member.
Grade:	Easy.

Points of Interest:

1.   Pennard cliffs stretch from Pwlldu Head to Three Cliffs Bay. Their limestone heights are of great archaeological, geological and historic interest, with Pwlldu Head the highest headland of Gower. Two of Gower's 'bone' caves lie close by. Limestone naturally lends itself to cave formation, and Gower's southern limestone edge is pitted with caves, and with rock faces of great appeal to climbers. In prehistory Gower's cliffs would have been much inland; the Bristol Channel then a river winding through a flat plain. Gower's limestone caves, at the edge of the great ice sheets, would have offered shelter to both early man and the animals he competed with for prey across a Britain still attached to the European continent. Minchin (marked Mitchin on OS maps) Hole, the nearest to the car park, was first excavated by a Colonel Ward in 1850. Finds, including bones of the narrow necked rhinoceros and straight tusked elephant, and of the mammoth and woolly rhinoceros, indicate usage over two climate stages; the first a temperate interglacial stage, the second indicating a much cooler climate. The bones would have been dragged there by hyenas or wolves. It is one of the few Gower caves where lion bones have been found. Bacon Hole, further to the east, was thought for a time to have

been, like the caves of Altamira in Spain, home to early prehistoric artists. In 1912 horizontal bands of dark red colour were discovered at the back of the cave. Believing these to be evidence of cave painting no less an expert than the Abbé Breuil, doyen of French prehistory, was brought in, who commented ' . . . *they could be'*. An iron grille, now fallen apart, was placed in front of them. However over the years the markings changed shape and the paintings were revealed as the natural seepings of iron oxide. As 'compensation' a bowl found on the site did reveal it as consistent with prehistoric man. Bones found include bison, giant ox, wolf, hyena, soft nosed rhinoceros, reindeer and straight tusked elephant – these can be seen at Swansea museum. Both caves are accessible from paths which run along the base of the cliffs between Fox Hole and Deep Slade, though neither are easy to find and will involve some scrambling.

At the western end of Pennard cliffs are Three Cliffs Bay and Pobbles Bay. Three Cliffs Bay takes it's name from the three linked and pointed cliffs overlooking the storm beach of Pobbles. The cliffs are bisected by a wide arch which gives access to the beach from Pennard pill, and whose rocky outcrops provide popular challenges to local climbers. Pennard cliffs as a whole were acquired by the National Trust in 1954 and are, like much National Trust land in Gower, common grazing ground. Southgate has grown much over the years, and now

Pennard Castle

110

spreads out to back the cliffs both sides of the starting point.

2. Despite having the finest site for castles in Gower, Pennard Castle is a shell. It was probably constructed at the end of the 13th century; possibly on the site of an earlier Danish stronghold. The ruins of the parish church are still discernible close by, buried in sand. Climate is never constant, and the fate of the castle and church seems to have been sealed in the 14th century. The coast during the 14th and 15th centuries was subject to ferocious gales, with the sands set in motion over huge areas; stabilisation of the dunes here did not take place until Tudor times. Like villages and churches along the coast, Pennard's castle and church became buried in the drifts of sand – the great and famous storm of 1607 seems to have finally sealed Pennard's fate. One popular folk legend has the Lord of Pennard and his followers' mouths, ears and eyes sealed by sand following transgression against the world of fairie; with a mountain of sand from Ireland suddenly disappearing at the same time. Pennard's church is now safe inland, and though probably dating from the 14th century only became the parish church when the older cliff church became buried. The rich maritime grassland of Pennard cliffs, including Pennard Castle, plays host to some rare alpine flora; just below the castle is a rare alpine found in Britain only in Gower.

Walk Directions   [-] denotes Point of Interest

1. Starting from Southgate car park [1] take the path leading right, initially passing in front of houses, then continuing along the cliff edge. Path well defined.

2. Follow the path until it descends to reach the valley path leading down to Pobbles beach and Three Cliffs Bay. Choice of routes down to valley.

3. From the valley take the boardwalk leading up on the right and continue, skirting the golf course, to reach the ruins of Pennard Castle [2]. Good views over Pennard pill below.

4. Follow the path from the castle to reach houses. Bear right on a waymarked path. The wooded path ahead will take you down to Parkmill. Follow the path as it skirts property boundaries and the water tower to reach a track. Stay right, on the track, to join the main road through Southgate.

5. Cross the main road, go up steps to the school entrance, and follow

the path through the kissing gates on the right as it follows the school perimeter.

6. Once at a stile cross three fields keeping to the left edge. At the end of the third field cross a stile left and bear right along the right edge of three more fields. Three-quarters of the way along the hedge of the third field is a stile giving access to Heol Lane.

7. Continue ahead on the road to reach the starting point.

Facilities

Most available in Southgate – shop, toilets and phone box by car park. The beach at Three Cliffs Bay, with it's strong currents, can be treacherous for bathers. Pennard golf course.

Caswell Bay – Brandy Cove – Hareslade – Bishopston Valley – Pwlldu – Brandy Cove – Caswell Bay

OS Maps:	OS Maps: 1:50 000 Swansea & Gower 159; Explorer 10 Gower.
Start:	Caswell Bay.
Access:	Caswell Bay is on the B4593 from Oystermouth (Ystumllwyniarth) and Mumbles. Buses from Swansea (Abertawe) Mondays to Saturdays stop close by.
Parking:	Car park at Caswell Bay – seasonal charge April to September.
Grade:	Moderate – Bishopston valley can be muddy after rains!

Points of Interest:

1.   Fringed by pine trees Caswell Bay is one of Gower's most popular beaches, popular with day trippers and surfers looking for the wilder waves that sweep into the bay. The bay's name derives from the small stream that runs down to the sea; the cress stream. Caswell marks the boundary of the old borough of Swansea Corporation, and it is the corporation that widened and metalled the cliff path from here on to Langlands Bay and Limeslade. It is one of the best loved walks in Gower, with walkers parking at Limeslade and Bracelet Bay near Mumbles Head to take the hour or so route over to Caswell. Bishop's Wood nature reserve, to the back of the bay, offers a fine variation of habitat for those seeking the cooler shades of the trees on those hot summer days.

2.   Bishopston valley is 2¹/₂ miles/4 kilometres long, the stream rising on the millstone grit of Fairwood Common. Once it reaches the limestone it initially sinks underground, only to re-emerge again half-way down the valley. The valley takes it's name from nearby Bishopston, with it's fine late 12th/13th century sheltered church – the manor originally belonged to the Bishop of Llandaff. In terms of woodland history the valley is ancient, with cover going back at least

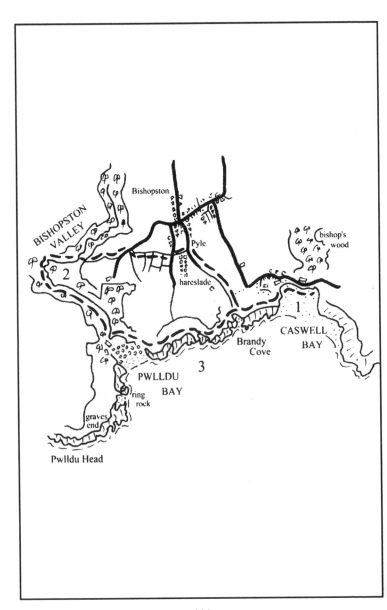

Bishopston

BISHOPSTON VALLEY

bishop's wood

Pyle

2

hareslade

1

CASWELL BAY

Brandy Cove

3

PWLLDU BAY

ring rock

graves end

Pwlldu Head

five hundred years, if not back to the Ice Age of some 10,000 years ago. Small scale 17th to 19th century quarries and limekilns dot the valley with, towards the Kittle and church end, the 18th/19th century silver lead mine now a sheltered home for the bats!

3. The Welsh name Pwlldu (Black Pool), unusual in the by now predominantly English place names of south Gower, derives from the pool formed by the outflow of the Bishopston stream as it reaches the ridge of the finest storm beach in Gower, the limestone pebbled beach of Pwlldu Bay (the pebbles are leftover waste from the quarrying). The stream only breaks though to the sea after heavy rains give it the power to impose. Like all Gower's prominent headlands Pwlldu Head, Gower's highest at some 300 feet/97 metres, was quarried for limestone in the 19th century. Trenches, or 'slides', serrate the headland down to Pwlldu Bay, where limestone blocks were slid down the cliff on wooden sledges for export to the waiting ships bound for north Devon and Cornwall. Ring Rock, close to the foreshore, was a popular tying up point. Of the now private houses by the beach one was once the Beaufort Inn, serving both quarrymen and the sailors who

Caswell Bay

frequented the busy port. Place names often give indication of significant landscape or historic features; just below Pwlldu Head is Graves End. In 1760 the press-gangs had been out 'recruiting' for the Royal Navy, and in November of that year the *Caesar* had been transporting some eighty press-ganged men, many from Bristol, from Swansea to Plymouth. With weather deteriorating the vessel, mistaking Pwlldu Head for Mumbles Head and shelter, turned inland only to be wrecked on the rocks. With the press-ganged men either shut in or handcuffed to the timbers below, there were few survivors. Some, depending on tradition, sixty-eight to ninety-seven, men were washed ashore and buried in a mass grave commemorated only by the name.

During the 18th and early 19th century Pwlldu and neighbouring Brandy Cove (originally called Hareslade until the name was changed during the Napoleonic wars) was one of the major smuggling centres of Gower. Often called the Kings of the Gower smugglers the Arthurs, father and son, lived at Great Highway on the Pennard to Southgate road, with their lieutenant John Griffiths living almost opposite at Little Highway. The two houses acted as storehouses and distribution centre for the goods landed at the two beaches, with pack horses (borrowed farm horses) carrying them up the Bishopston valley and Smugglers Lane by Widegate. Lundy Island, out in the Bristol Channel, was the centre for much of the smuggling, with landings of brandy and wine from France and salt, soap, tea and tobacco from Ireland, and coastal traders would land to pick up goods for transfer to Pwlldu Bay, often in broad daylight. Needless to say the Arthurs owned their own vessels – as the owner of quarries on Swansea canal, William Arthur (son) had legitimate reasons for their ownership! A large operation could involve as many as a hundred men, enough to curb the fire of any Customs official. The tide only began to turn against the smugglers in 1804 when Customs officers, with help from the local Glamorgan Sea Fencibles (volunteer organisations formed to resist any Napoleonic invasion), surprised landings at Great and Little Highway, and seized nearly three thousand gallons of spirits. With further seizures from 1804 onwards, smuggling became small scale and took place during darkness. By 1850 it had been largely destroyed; with free trade customs duties were no longer so high, and the risks were now too great.

Walk Directions   [-] denotes Point of Interest

1. Starting from Caswell Bay **[1]** cross the beach and ascend the steps leading up from the embankment below the modern flats to Redley Cliff. If the tide is well in there are paths leading off from the road to Bishopston which will give access.

2. Continue on the coastal path around the cliff to Brandy Cove.

3. At Brandy Cove turn right, away from the coast, on a well defined path, and continue ahead as the path becomes a track and then a road.

4. Just after passing a sign on the left for Hareslade, turn left onto a path. Walking man sign here.

5. Continue on the path to meet a minor road. Cross the road and follow the track across football fields, passed the clubhouse, and from the fourth field cross right a smaller field to meet a minor road.

6. Turn left onto the road and after a short distance keep ahead on a green lane to shortly descend downhill on a path by metal gates.

7. Continue downhill ignoring paths on left and right to Bishopston valley floor **[2]**.

8. Cross the stone footbridge, turn left, and follow riverside paths to reach Pwlldu **[3]**.

9. Cross the footbridge over the Bishopston stream and continue uphill on a track. After a short distance, as the landscape opens up, turn right off the track onto the lower coastal path.

10. Continue on the coastal path to Brandy Cove, and on back to Caswell Bay and the starting point.

Facilities

> BT telephone, toilets and beach shops at Caswell Bay. Also lifeguard phone. Bishop's Wood nature reserve and centre close by, as is the nature reserve at Redley Cliff.

More Walking Books ....

Visit our website for further information:
www.carreg-gwalch.com

Orders can be placed on our
On-line Shop